CHRISTIAN
WARRIOR
WOMEN

CHRISTIAN
WARRIOR
WOMEN

A Guide To Taking Back Your Faith, Family & Future

LISA HAWKINS

Christian Warrior Women Publishing

Published in Atlanta, Georgia by Christian Warrior Women Publishing

Unless otherwise stated, scriptures are taken from the Holy Bible, New International Version

ISBN 978-0-692-12064-4

Printed in the United States of America

First Printing, 2018

Dedication

*This book is dedicated to the loving memories and prayers that gave
me the confidence and strength to fight and rise up in faith as a
daughter of God. My grandmother Zilpha Cooper's prayers, my
mother and confidant Maxine Edgecombe, and my father Samuel
Hampton for my inspiration.*

*May Jesus continue to shine His blessings upon your lives, my
husband Andre Hawkins Sr. and my sons Andre Hawkins Jr.,
Daniel J. Hawkins, and Amiri H. Hawkins.
Thank you…*

Warrior Women TF 2015-2016

*To all the women God brought through the first twenty-four weeks
of Warrior Women TF training sessions.*

*Each of you gave me the strength and courage to make this book
a reality.*

*Special shout out to Mrs. Kimberly Yontz and Ms. Vanessa
Armorer for your obedience to God.*

*Jody Freeman, thanks for being chosen by God to be the
encouraging force for my voice to be heard.*

*Thank you to everyone who has served in Open Heaven Healing
Rooms, Atlanta, with special acknowledgement to: Mrs. Erecilla
Mims, Ms.Stacy Savage, and Ms. Molly Welsh.*

Romans 8:37
**"In all these things, we are more than conquerors through Him who
loved us."**

Table of Contents

Preface

Christian Warrior Women:
A Guide to Taking Back Your Faith,
Family, & Future

Welcome to the training that was inspired by God to bring revelation, healing, and miracles to a generation of women in need of a Savior.

In her ministry work, Lisa Hawkins—ordained minister, missionary, entrepreneur, Christian Coach, Georgia State Director of International Association of Healing Rooms and founder of Warrior Women Task Force in 2015, shares her life mission to make women fearless through healing and identity.

In her own life, Lisa has overcome many fierce challenges: childhood molestation, divorce, sexual harassment, racism, single motherhood, and more. She has risen to embrace her identity, as a woman of color who fought to shatter the glass ceiling at top international consumer product companies, and battled for her personal, professional, and spiritual goals.

Lisa works with women through the Warrior Women Ministry and other healing groups, and now she's sharing her teachings with you in, *Christian Warrior Women: Taking Back Your Faith, Family & Future*. Her teachings, rooted in her own pursuit of a relationship with God and her own healing, helps women arm themselves for battle ... to fight for their lives and unlock their potential for a better life—a better marriage, a better family life, professional and financial success, deeper friendships, and more. Lisa's inspired lessons will teach you how. She will help you;

- Acknowledge the destructive layers of false belief, pain, and fear that prevent you from seeing your true self, as God sees you.
- Uncover the root of when and why these false beliefs, pain, and fear started.
- Stop sabotaging your relationships, career, and finances.
- Break free from the bondage of your past and pave a new exciting journey.
- Overcome the negative patterns set in motion by abuse, addiction, rejection, illness, abandonment, unworthiness and shame.
- Develop a relationship with God that's soulful and impactful and helps you gain the confidence you need to embrace your true God-given identity, gifts, and talents.
- Accept the Warrior Mantle God gave you as Adam's strongest companion and equip yourself with the strategies and tactics of the Christian Warrior Woman that God created you to be. You are in the battle for YOUR life, and God wants you to win!

A word from Lisa:

If you're ready to become a Warrior Woman and fight for your life, then this book will show you how to prepare for battle. God made it clear He wanted me to share how I broke free of rejection, abandonment, control, soul ties, shame, and generational patterns.

You can't be a Warrior Woman unless you decide that your life and impact on your family and community is worth fighting for. You can't win the battles on your own; that's why you need a Savior. You gain experience in battle on how to advance against your enemy. You learn your weaknesses and strengths.

Let's turn your lost battles of the past into conquering your obstacles of the future. We can't fix the past, but we shall clear the path ahead. You may have felt lost and off course for a long time. That's about to change.

When I searched for my identity, I found it. That's doesn't make me perfect. It makes me humble and aware of who created me and for what purpose.

Be inspired by Ephesians 6:10-13, The Armor of God:

"Finally, be strong in the Lord and in His mighty power. Put on the full armor of God, so that you can take your stand against the devil's schemes. For our struggle is not against flesh and blood, but against the rulers, against the authorities, against the power of this dark world and against spiritual forces of evil in the heavenly realms. Therefore, put on the full armor of God, so that when the day of evil comes, you may be able to stand your ground, and after you have done everything, to stand."

Stand firm!

CHRISTIAN WARRIOR WOMEN

A Guide to Taking Back Your Faith, Family & Future

Introduction

Have you started believing that you can't recover from the mistakes of the past? Did your Plan A fail? Has divorce or single parenting left you emotionally and financially defeated? Are you single and losing hope on finding Mr. Right?

Today, many women are the heads of their households. Although there have been many advancements in female-owned companies and even a few CEOs of large corporations, there are still a multitude of challenges facing many women in areas such as: gender bias and wage discrepancy, equal rights, education, sexual harassment, drugs, and social pressures of meeting the needs of your children, and lastly, the role social media plays in how women receive affirmation.

The world continues to make women scrutinize their outward beauty, piece by piece. It's a self-hate formula to drive profits in the beauty category and lower the esteem of our young girls about their weight, height, shape, skin, eyes, butt, hair, lips, legs, and arms. With money and greed as the driving force, women will continue feeling insecure about their unique beauty in days to come. I can share one thing that hasn't changed: God's love and protection of his handmade "woman."

Do you find yourself losing sleep, worried about tomorrow, and gaining weight? That's not a place of strength for a daughter of God. If you often feel out of control, lonely, unappreciated, tired, depressed, unworthy, abandoned, self-sabotaging, and shame, I have a solution for you that will change your life.

In my past, I've spent a significant amount of time trying to undo, fix, or make up for my past instead of putting my energies into moving forward. Spending time mourning over the past, living in regret, and trying to make up for the past keeps you in a pattern of circling a dead situation. It took me too long to look ahead. I am here to be that voice that says, "Your good news is not going to come from your past, but from the future you run to meet!"

'Christian Warrior Women' is not for women who want to stand around whining and complaining about what's happened to them.

'Christian Warrior Women' is for women who want to know what God's plans are for them. God has plans that outnumber our calculators. Have you seen the stars in the heavens? It doesn't matter how many mistakes you've made or horrible things you've done. I promise you, God's Plan B is the *best* plan.

Women can learn how to take their lives back and bring healing to their thoughts, beliefs, and actions in ways they never thought possible. Christian Warrior Women challenges the victim mentality that many women embrace over time. Many women have early or current traumatic experiences that need healing. We can learn, gain strength, knowledge, and perseverance in troubling times or we can become a prisoner of the past.

Christian Warrior Women focuses on what is the truth and who can be impacted and set free with the knowledge about God in their lives. We all get knocked down, but we must get up again and again. You must believe that your life is worth fighting for. Christian Warrior Women will help you love and accept yourself with all your flaws. You are the only you upon the whole earth.

You are worth the journey of fulfillment.

What motivated me to write this book? After twenty-five years in corporate America as an executive for top corporations and the first or only female of color in every position, I made a choice for my family. I never knew that choice would lead to a journey proving God was real and that He really loved me.

Ten years after serving in the healing ministry and helping other men and women find their purpose, God called me a Warrior in prayer one day. The Lord asked me to share what I had experienced in my own healing and witnessed in my relationship with Him.

Even though I was an ordained minister and had served in many ministries, missionary work in South Africa, the Navajo Nation, and other areas, I wasn't interested or eager to take the Lord's assignment. I gave Him reasons why other people would be better suited. I said I never wanted to work in women's ministry. The Lord laughed at me and reminded me that I was already working in women's ministry and had been for years — in prisons, youth detention, as a small group leader, through my own ministry at Open Heaven Healing Rooms, and three other ministries.

Shortly after the prayer, the Lord had two ministers give me a prophetic word; neither had any idea what was said in my private talks with God nor what He had told me to do. I had been in training with one of the ministers in 2010 at Life Center Church. We were all eager and excited to learn and be activated in healing, deliverance, miracles, and prophetic training. This friend was currently on staff at Life Center Church.

The Lord knew I would trust the word coming from Pastor Samuel Giles. He said that the Lord was bringing women around me to mentor, train, and activate. As they were speaking, it felt like an emotional explosion was going off inside of me. In all honesty, I really didn't want to hear it so clearly.

He then continued. I would sound the alarm for the Warriors of God. They would be raised up to perform signs and wonders. Kingdom women would know their identities. If you go on our website, you can hear the prophetic word that confirmed God's choice for me to start Warrior Women in 2015. After two different, clear messages from God, do you think I could escape or tell God "no" any longer?

Within a month, my first class began. I could not believe the impact God was having on the lives of the women. With every new session, the classes grew into blessings and miracles beyond my thoughts or imagination. Warrior Women Task Force started out as an eight-week training course that turned into twenty-four weeks.

Women were hearing about the class and wanted to attend. Women started asking me to write a book because this was something that seasoned Christian leaders were receiving healing, power, and authority activated in their lives. The eight weeks felt like a Boot Camp with Jesus.

It can be tough, but the rewards are limitless. It's a journey that is guaranteed to over-deliver on your expectations. You make the choice to step out on faith and let Jesus do the rest. I was there to support, coach, cheer, and facilitate the participants to keep focused on Christ and their future.

Here are a couple of scriptures to encourage you to move forward with God:

Isaiah 58:11 - *"The Lord will guide me continually."*

Psalms 23:1 - *"God will show me the path of life."*

What I love about the Old Testament is that when God allowed Moses to set the children of Israel free from bondage from Pharaoh and the Egyptians, they still had to fight and war against others to get to their Promised Land. As Christian women, we sometimes sit back and wait for the parting sea or life to come to us. The Israelites had to go through some battles to reach their promise.

The promise begins with *your* belief then actions. God gave us power and authority to speak our future into existence. Life is full of struggles no matter who you are. If you do not have the tools as a woman of faith, you will fail in this life. *Christian Warrior Women* will provide the tools and skills to make you that impactful woman.

One day before teaching a Warrior Women class (third group, twenty-two weeks later), I prayed, "Lord, if you really want me to do this on a larger scale as a career, give me a sign." One hour later, a woman attending the class approached me, nervous and shaking. I asked if she was all right.

She handed me an envelope and began telling me how the Lord instructed her to give it to me. A bit surprised, I asked, "What do you mean?

She answered, "If I give you this, the Lord is going to bless me greatly."

She then told me she had to go to two ATMs. I opened the envelope to find it was full of money.

"It's one thousand dollars," she said,

"in twenty-dollar bills."

Truly confused, I replied,

"I don't know what you mean."

She looked at me and said, "Lisa, the Lord told me you needed a sign to take Warrior Women global."

Stunned, I asked, "*What* did you say?!"

She repeated it again. My heart skipped a beat because no one knew what I'd prayed an hour earlier. I've had many God encounters, but I wasn't expecting this response so quickly.

The words were barely out of my mouth when the Lord told her to get the money. Are you kidding me?

My Journey

I believe the Lord changed me into a true Warrior Woman during the experience I am about to share.

I was working for PepsiCo, and they moved me from Charlotte, North Carolina, where my first son was born to Winston-Salem, North Carolina. The move came after the first set of racial jokes, slurs, and the N-word were used by a franchise bottler and shared with my peers behind my back. The company never addressed it or supported me by saying the behavior was unacceptable.

There was one African American executive who was trying to help me, but at the time, it was very stressful. He was mentoring me and felt moving me to Winston-Salem would make things better. It didn't make things better. I, not the disrespectful franchise bottler, was perceived as the problem. Ignoring the unacceptable behavior brought more pain, stress, sexism, and discrimination than I had ever seen or would experience in my life.

Months after the move, we drove to Charlotte to visit family and friends. I woke up feeling like I was coming down with the flu. I didn't want to go, but I knew we had made plans. I never get headaches, but that day my head was pounding. We always put AJ in the back seat of the Pontiac Bonneville. AJ cried that day to be in the front passenger seat with his dad. I told him he couldn't.

AJ started crying that he wanted to be near his daddy. My head was throbbing, so I agreed for a little while, hoping my head would stop hurting. We moved his car seat to the front passenger seat, and I laid out in the back seat with the overwhelming headache.

We weren't two miles from the house when the car hit a crack in the road and started spinning out of control. Andre began yelling, "Oh, my God!" I saw we were heading across the median into oncoming traffic on I-40.

I had no seat belt on in the back, and I was trying to reach for my son in the passenger's seat. Andre was yelling at what was ahead of us, and I was focused on stabilizing AJ in his car seat. We kept getting banged around because we hit over ten cars on the other side with oncoming traffic. I could barely reach AJ, and I ignored Andre's yelling.

The cars hitting us kept knocking me down to the backseat floor. I had my arm stretched towards AJ's head. Then there was a yell from Andre, "This is it, oh my God, a bus!" I looked up and saw a Greyhound bus coming toward us for a head-on collision, and again I thought of AJ in the front. The next thing I knew was that the car hit something, went spinning, and came to a stop.

I remember in those moments Andre saying, "No." I accepted I had no control, and this was the end. I remember the car being banged, hit, and then saying, "It is finished." In that moment, I believed my life was over. I heard someone from outside say, "I am a doctor." They were trying to get Andre out, who was stuck in the driver's seat.

I passed out in the back (I believe) shortly after somebody opened the back door. As I was sprawled out on the floor in the back seat I saw my son, AJ, outside the car, lying face up on the grass. Then I saw someone pulling a blanket over his body and head. I screamed or thought, "NOOOOOOOOO!!! My son is dead."

I passed out.

The next thing I knew, I was in an empty, grey garage in the late afternoon. I was on a middle level, but there were no cars in the garage. It was like a large concrete, multi-level parking structure that should have an elevator.

I was there alone. I started calling for my dad. I said, "Daddy, I'm here. Daddy, where are you?" There was no answer; nobody was there. I started walking. When the accident happened, my father had been dead for five years. I heard no answer. I wondered why he wasn't answering me.

There were no sounds, no people; just a plain concrete garage with no cars. I felt comfortable. I wasn't scared. I just wanted my dad to know I was there. Then a voice that sounded like my dad said, "Go back."

I replied, "I don't want to go back."

I heard my dad's voice saying,

"You *must* go back."

I had no thoughts of what "go back" meant in the garage. I had no memory of my child or anything I had left behind. I was fine where I was. I had no knowledge of anything going on anywhere else. The voice came closer and felt warmer, although the garage didn't change.

The voice said, "It's not your time.

You must go back."

I could feel the voice sending me into *something*. I hope I can describe this, but the closest thing to help you understand is for you to imagine a colorful bubble portal. I fell through a vacuum funnel of lights and colors, and I didn't feel the weight of my body. I wasn't traveling in my physical body. It was my spirit traveling.

I then entered an ambulance, above myself on the gurney, with the EMT. I could see my body, but I was in the corner ceiling of the ambulance, hovering over and looking at the EMT working on me. The EMT in the back yelled to the driver, "Hurry, we are losing her!"

I saw him get a big needle and hit my chest with it. I felt a jerk between the two pieces of me. I realized my spirit and my body were separate. The EMT looked worried and scared and was pounding on my chest. I was observing this with no emotional attachment.

I felt my spirit enter my body which is hard to describe, except the spirit which is the life force and light collided with something solid – flesh and blood – entered and became alive. It was like a splash into experience. My spirit plunged into my body and brought it to life.

I was in my body, looking at the EMT as he was pounding on my chest, telling others he was losing me. I tried to tell him, "No, you are not, I'm here." I was yelling, and yet he couldn't hear me. I didn't understand why they couldn't see my eyes open or my mouth or lips moving. I kept yelling, "Dude, I'm right here! Stop hitting my chest and look at me!"

We arrived at the hospital, and as they were removing me from the ambulance, the EMT told the doctors I was unstable, that he was losing me, and had given me meds. Then out of nowhere, they heard me say, "I'm right here. Can't you hear me?"

The EMT finally said, "Wow, you are back. Thank goodness."

I said, "I have *been* here, trying to tell you all!" They wheeled me into an emergency room. When the nurse rolled me in, there was so much hustle and stress from all the people involved in the accident.

They were attaching oxygen and other tubes all over me when I asked for my son. They told me that I-40 was shut down, due to helicopters and ambulance people trying to get to the various hospitals.

- I said, "I must find my son." I was beginning to regain the memory of seeing him with a blanket over his head.
- I asked again, "Where is my son?"
- They said something like, "Get her something to calm her."
- I said it louder. "WHERE IS MY SON?!"

Through all the noise of the emergency room, I heard a child crying out from what the doctors were doing to him. I heard my son.

I said, "AJ, Mommy is here!"

I got up, pushed the nurse away, snatched the IV out, and ran across the ER looking for AJ. I bumped into Andre, looking all banged up, and I asked him if he had seen AJ. He answered, "No."

The nurses shouted, "Ma'am, come back!"

AJ cried out again as I reached him. My son was alive, and that was all that mattered to me. I asked, "How is he?"

They didn't know at that point.

The nurses and doctors stated, "You are in worse shape than your son."

My arm was bleeding where the IV had been, but I told them I would not leave my son's side. They informed me that I would have to sign papers stating I'd refused help. I told them to get whatever I needed to sign, but I was not leaving his side.

As I watched them help AJ, I overheard how the driver of the Greyhound bus full of passengers about to hit us head on made a split-second move. If he hadn't, he could have killed the passengers on that bus and us.

The Greyhound bus driver was the hero. Andre was wheeled over, and he said he thought we were dead. After we had hit ten cars or more, the Greyhound bus driver had swerved to avoid us. Everyone was stating it was a miracle that we hit so many cars and made it out alive.

The doctor came and requested that I be looked after. I then heard the nurse stated,

"She flatlined in the ambulance."

I was trying to figure out how I had flatlined but had been in a garage. AJ was my priority, but my dad had spoken to me in the garage and told me to come back. I remembered, "You must go back. It's not your time."

The doctors wanted to keep AJ for observation because his blood pressure was low, and they wanted to run some tests. We stayed by his side until evening. After the tests, they believed AJ had internal bleeding and wanted to do surgery immediately. We approved.

They had to cut away six inches of AJ's bowels due to the internal bleeding; the seat belt damage his intestines and cut off blood flow. AJ looked pale and tired, but he was alive and recovering. He was only four years old when he had to be cut open. My only son was alive and looked so weak.

I was grateful God intervened and saved our lives. My Grandmother Cooper prayed for her daughter and grandchildren three times a day. Her prayers and relationship with God spared our lives. Remembering the words "Go back" was life changing.

My grandmother, Lula Hampton, who was my father's mother, told my dad to never let me live in the south. She told him it would kill me. A part of me died that day in Winston-Salem, North Carolina.

I didn't know the woman that came back from the garage would become a Warrior Woman. She would come back focused, determined to fight against racial discrimination at PepsiCo, change jobs, relocate, triple her income in three years, twice adopt African American sons in years to come, and gain her professional and spiritual identity.

No longer did I work at representing blacks, women, or any other group. I came back representing Lisa C. Hawkins, her career, and her family aspirations. I was driven to conquer everything I set my mind to.

The woman that came back left the victim, stress, struggles of her youth in that empty garage. I didn't know where I was headed, but we moved to Colorado shortly with a new company and I found God's love in Denver.

What I didn't know was that with my new confidence, I had entered a war at a new level. Little did I know that it would take more than my willpower to overcome the battle and spiritual warfare that was headed my way. The awakening had begun around me, but the struggle ahead for me and my sons was far from over. God knew what He'd created me to do, but was I equipped and ready?

I am here to tell you it's time for *your* awakening. Your eyes, ears, and spiritual consciousness are going to allow you the opportunity to conquer fear and overcome the adversity that is plaguing you and your family

.

Battle Zone

1. Think of a life experience that was
    a turning point in your life.

_____

_____

_____

_____

_____

2. What did you learn about yourself?

_____

_____

_____

_____

_____

3. Describe the pros/cons of the change.

_____

_____

_____

_____

_____

4. What change do you need in your
    life right now?

_____

_____

_____

_____

I found God after being tired of failing at fixing my own life and circumstances. I am the youngest child of six, raised by a single mom in New York City. I endured things I vowed my children would never experience in their lives. At a young age, I felt abandoned, unwanted, and unworthy. As I got older, despair would hunt me down through disappointment, loneliness, heartbreak, and other life-threatening events.

Despite the challenges of my childhood, I went on to attend a great college, Syracuse University. My career landed me in top corporations, holding positions as the first woman and African American in management in several top consumer products companies, with sales and manufacturing responsibilities. It sounds great on paper, but given the level of sexism and racism I endured, if I had to do it again, would I? No.

Time was wasted simply proving I was equal as a woman or smart enough as a black person to hold the position. The corporate loneliness, isolation, and effects on my health today directly correlate to how hard I had to fight to not let corporate break me. I was representing the future of women and blacks. After the accident, I decided I *was representing me*, and that's when my career took off.

In this book, I will share my experiences and those of other women who made the choice to trust God in all things. You will see Jesus and the Holy Spirit showing up often throughout the book to defend and protect me and my family. You will reflect and learn that Jesus has done the same for you. Hold on to your skirts and hair extensions. It's going to feel like a rollercoaster at times.

This book is the first in a series written to bring the armor of faith and strategies filled with hope and light for your future with the wisdom of peace from Christ.

The *Christian Warrior Women* book will help you:

- Gain direction on the steps to a fulfilling relationship with God that's intimate, personal, impactful, and will help you gain the confidence you need to embrace your true God-given identity, gifts, and talents.
- Learn how God released the Warrior Mantle upon Eve as the competent (handmade) companion for Adam. Eve was equipped with additional skills to defeat the future schemes of the enemy.

- Acknowledge the repetitive patterns of disappointments, insecurity, unworthiness, shame, heartbreak, doubts, control, and fears that prevent you from seeing the beautiful woman God created.
- Uncover the root of when your false beliefs and fear began.
- Identify how you are sabotaging your relationships, career, and finances.
- Break free from the bondage of heartbreak (soul-ties) and pave a new exciting journey.
- Learn how to overcome the negative patterns set in motion by ancestral patterns.
- Impact your community, nation, and generations to come by faith.
- See Jesus as a Defender of women.

In reflecting on God calling me to be a Warrior, I realized that everything I had achieved in my life came through perseverance, trust, and faith in my darkest hours. Christ was by my side even when I felt alone in the war.

I wrote this book because I want you to have the tools to fight for your life with the full understanding of who you are as a woman and God's plan for you. The war comes as daily battles against you in areas of trust in your relationships with God, family, and people in the workplace, and regarding your health.

Life is about overcoming struggles and battling with the power and authority given to you by the blood of Jesus Christ. That sounds good, but how it's activated and implemented in daily life can be confusing. I am going to make it simple for you. The struggles cannot be overcome by hoping, wishing, or waiting to be rescued. Rather, *you* can overcome them if you are grounded in the knowledge of the truth and faith.

The Christian Warrior Women Book

This book is an exciting daily, weekly, Christian spiritual journey of real life, in-your-face showdowns of the miraculous work of Jesus in the flesh and in the spirit realm. Each chapter will have engaging, exciting, intense, emotional moments of a real woman's life that you will experience that will allow you to see God clearly operating.

This view will also provide an opportunity for you to see how He has been operating in your life. You will be spiritually inspired with an impact upon your faith, and shocked at the level of engagement Jesus has prepared for you. He is going to make you a change agent in areas in which you feel defeated.

How It Begins

The first chapter opens in the hospital ER with flashback memories of over thirty-five years prior. Imagine having your most painful buried experiences brought back to full memory. The memories and the experiences since 2005 comprise the teachings and learnings for the *Christian Warrior Women* series.

Each chapter of the book will be set up in three parts:

- Key scriptures: relevant to the chapters
- Warrior Life Examples: examples relevant to the chapters
- Battle Zones: Self-reflections
    a. Questions and self-revelations about your healing needs, and others, as well as how to take back what's been robbed, stolen or destroyed within the subject
    b. Resources to connect you with support

The book will motivate you to begin the journey of a Christian Warrior Woman. Get some girlfriends together, or a small group at work or church, and be committed to support each other. Meet weekly and be united in faith together. It doesn't matter where you are on the faith scale today.

Small Focus Group

It's not easy to face your fears. The real work happens in the weekly exercises of walking out your healing. When you meet weekly with your group, you will need a leader/facilitator to organize the weekly gathering, the exercises, and discussion topics in the book. There will be online training for those who want to facilitate leading women to step up to become Warriors.

Connect with me on Facebook, Twitter, and/or through the website. (www.christianwarriorwomen.com).

Encouraging Word

As you read this book, the scales will fall from your eyes and the callousness from your heart as you explore family and living dynamics in a new way. You will be asked to dive deep within your emotional pool of life experiences, flush out the waste, and acknowledge how the Lord's saving grace brought you through.

Women have a special connection to God, Jesus, and the Holy Spirit. You will learn why.

When you buy a bicycle or anything that must be assembled, you get directions. The directions provide the steps of how the item should be assembled and the best ways to use it. If you assemble it on your own without following the directions, it may not work properly, or you won't get the item's full benefits. The warranty may also be voided if the directions are not followed.

This book will lead you to understand how God created, purchased, and paid the highest price possible with the blood of Jesus Christ. He made you for such a time as this, with the characteristics and circumstances you have experienced, to conquer and win.

When a product doesn't work properly it needs to be returned to the manufacturer. Will you return to your Creator and become the leader and overcomer you were called to be? Your life may be a mess today, but there is "now" for a change.

Isn't it time you read the directions (the Bible) and call customer service (Jesus) to discuss how you can sign up for the full lifetime coverage warranty? The policy has already been paid for, and the call is toll free with no cellular or data charges. You can't get a better deal than that, my friend.

Your future has been waiting for you long enough. Women globally are gaining the power of their united voices and beginning to expose the devil's schemes and lies that have kept them hidden in darkness from their identity and purpose. For too long, women have accepted broken promises, failure, remorse, poverty, discrimination, low wages, sexual abuse, and lost faith in their future.

We were created to have authority and success against everything and anything that comes up against God's plan for our lives. Christ says, "No more." Scripture supports the equality of women from the beginning and in the last days:

"In the last days, God says, I will pour out my Spirit on all people. Your sons and daughters will prophesy, your young men will see visions, your old men will dream dreams." Acts 2:17

I am a daughter of God, and I prophesy that you will become a Christian Warrior Woman and take back your faith, family, and future in Jesus' name.

Chapter One

SHAME: The Struggle Buried Within

Isaiah 54:4
"Do not be afraid; you will not be put to shame.
Do not fear disgrace, you will not be humiliated.
You will forget the shame of your youth and remember no more the reproach of your
widowhood."

While I was living in Dallas, Texas. I accepted a position as Executive Group Vice President for a major food company that would require me to move to St. Louis, Missouri. At the time, my sons were in their first semester of high school in Dallas, Texas.

One of my sons was a top high school and AAU basketball player in the state and was ranked nationally. During the six months of interviews which started prior to my son's first semester in high school in Texas, I made it very clear that if I took the job and relocated to St. Louis, I would be unable to move again for the next three years. I would have to stay in St. Louis until they finished high school. My sons agreed to one move from Texas to Missouri only.

For my son, AJ, who played basketball, moving was a big deal as local high schools and AAU coaches were reaching out and requesting dinner to discuss possibilities. St. Louis rolled out the red carpet for my son, announcing the school he was to attend could win a state championship.

His first game in St. Louis was standing room only. I barely got in by announcing I was his mother! For my other son, Daniel, leaving his friends behind in Texas led him to go from an A student to a student who didn't care. My youngest was in Montessori School learning how to pour tea (he recalls this as his only memory).

While still living in relocation three weeks later, the company announced they were reorganizing and would be moving the offices to Downers Grove, Chicago. You can imagine my shock, dismay, and concern.

My oldest son, AJ, was now playing basketball for his new high school, one of the top teams in St. Louis. He had been featured in the newspaper and mentioned on the radio as a player who could help lead the team to the state championships. My middle son was not adapting well to St. Louis. He loved Texas and missed his friends.

I was a single mom with an ex-husband who lived with me to help with the kids because I traveled Monday through Thursday. It's common now, but it wasn't in the late 1990s to early 2000s. After a couple of meetings in which I stated I could not move to Chicago with three kids and three dogs —not to mention snow— it was agreed I could move to Atlanta. Atlanta was a place I never wanted to live. God had tried to get me there before, but I had refused.

Worse, I now had to face my children again and tell them I would be breaking my word. Prior to our move to St. Louis, my kids and I had already moved seven times. I had promised that once they entered high school, we wouldn't move again. St. Louis was supposed to be our home for the next three and a half years. How could I dare ask them to forgive me and move again?

AJ had already played his varsity freshman year at two schools and now would be playing at another one. In three semesters, he would have three coaches in three different states and three sets of players and friends. Daniel was already unhappy with one move, and my youngest was too young to care.

Things were spiraling out of control. I had told a friend when all my things were loaded on the two eighteen-wheeler trucks in Texas that something wasn't right. I told them I shouldn't move, that the money was a trick. They had never seen me fearful about a job before. I explained to them that I didn't have a good feeling about the move. I couldn't shake it. They reminded me that I'd never made that amount of money or taken on such responsibility either.

But I knew deep down it wasn't that. It has never been about money for me. It's always been about the challenge, the experience, and the opportunity. What would happen in St. Louis? I then knew my gut that never failed me was right. My inner voice told me, "Don't leave Texas!" I had avoided Atlanta many times.

As my family's breadwinner, what could I do? That's the question the CEO and President must have asked —and answered— when they'd recruited me. If I had known about the reorganization, I would have never left Colgate-Palmolive. The new company thought the money would make it right. Wrong!

I was deeply troubled because my sons were seriously not happy. They didn't want to leave Texas, and now they didn't want to leave their St. Louis school. When I met with the president of the company to whom I reported, he told me he "didn't know" about the reorganization.

I think a rage swelled in me; to claim he didn't know was ignorant. I didn't start until February, and the announcement was in March. I'd accepted the position back in November, so they had to have known something at that point. I was so angry and frustrated, and I felt manipulated. I was angry because I felt they wanted a woman of color, so they lied, believing the money would make it okay.

I started having severe migraine headaches. I had never had migraines in my life up until that time. I also realized I had reached my limit with corporate America, and my twenty years of fighting against discrimination and the rights as a woman had to stop.

Migraines Headaches & Flashes

In my rage about my personal circumstances, I tried to put on the best face for my kids, at work, at basketball games. I felt seriously ill. I didn't want them to see how upset and angry I was inside about breaking my word to them. I felt helpless and trapped because if I quit the company, I would be stuck in St. Louis until I found another job. Atlanta, at least, offered me closer proximity to family and the east, so I agreed to the move. While looking for housing in Atlanta, the migraine headaches continued.

A new job, two moves and severe migraines— not a good start. The headaches were so bad I was bedridden for days. My head felt like rockets were being launched inside it. During these headaches, I started to see flashes of myself as a little girl. I felt panic as I saw myself running. I saw myself having a conversation with a man, then a flashing, blinding light.

I would wake up panicked and sweating and would fall out of the bed. I realized that all my life, I had been running from something in my dreams. When I was about to be caught, I would have powers that protected me.

The headaches continued, with flashes of my past arising. I knew what I saw in these flashes was true because I felt a confirmation in my spirit that I knew the people, places, situations, and things said in these flashbacks.

I often saw myself in a dark room and would wake up shaking with fear. This continued, which led to sleepless nights. During this time, I felt manipulated. I had disappointed my sons, a boss had lied to me, and coworkers were apologizing for how the company had misled me. I had been here too many times before.

There was also another pressure: the CEO of my new company was the President of my division at PepsiCo when I worked there. She was directly responsible for not doing anything about my situation with the franchise bottler and the manager who had unleashed the most painful racism of my career. I sued the company over it. (That's a different book to look forward to.) I had taken a job where one of my worst nightmares had followed me. Could my life get any worse?

Unfortunately, yes it could.

In My Sleep

I was having the flashbacks when I was asleep or awake. Looking back now, I can see the plan was to make me remember the details. At the time, it was such a rush of my own memories and emotions. I was hearing and seeing someone familiar in a supernatural way, telling me as a child who I would become.

I had heard that voice before. Was that where my confidence came from? I knew the voice had been speaking to me my whole life, and I knew it from a special time long ago. That voice made a little girl a promise. Why did I feel safe with the voice?

I had reached the Group Vice President level that I'd prayed for so long ago. I saw myself in my twenties, praying to God that if He'd bless me to be a Vice President one day, I would give my life to helping people find Christ. I had knelt and made that prayer. Each word was my word I'd said many years earlier.

I heard a voice state, "It is that time."

But whose voice was I hearing? Why was my head full of memories I had forgotten? I'd made those promises and said those words. I had made it to the checkpoint. It was now time for me to make good on my words. What was I supposed to do?

We moved to Atlanta, and I was in the process of buying a home in the suburbs of Johns Creek, Georgia. My struggle with headaches and sleep continued while we lived in temporary housing in North Fulton, awaiting the closing of my house.

I decided to seek professional help. The psychologist I saw believed I was being shown something that my brain couldn't handle when the events had occurred. She told me that when we go through extremely painful experiences, the brain can block them to relieve stress.

She asked me to try to see where I was in the dark room when I was three or four years old. She tried to guide me through that memory, but I panicked during the session and started crying. I realized I felt trapped again. The psychologist asked what I meant. I described what I was experiencing at work, which reminded me of another time when I felt tricked, trapped, alone, and too small to do anything. I was seeing myself being locked in a room with an old man; the door closes, and I can't get out. I don't know what happened, only that it was too painful and horrible to remember.

I felt a flood of emotions as I left the psychologist's office. As I was driving to our hotel, the memories started coming faster, forcing me to remember words being said, running, and being afraid. I felt my chest pounding like I was going to faint. Why were these memories flooding my head now?

I drove myself to the nearest hospital. There, as I sat in the ER for over an hour, the Holy Spirit brought me flashes of childhood memories that changed my whole outlook on life, people, and God. What I'd experienced brought secrets, shame, fear, control, perfectionism, and abandonment. These strongholds had been at the root of my decisions my whole life. Why did God want me to relive and see the things I had shoved so deep within myself, so I could forget them?

Abandonment

I was three or four years old and living with strangers. In those days, I had no memories of my mother, except longing to see her. At the time, I didn't know why my mother or family kept me away. Maybe it was because she was a working single mom, beautiful, and trying to find Mr. Right? As for my father, I don't have any memories about him until I was five years old, at which time I went to live with my grandmother, Zilpha Cooper.

My mother had a woman care for me because she worked one to two jobs, and daycare wasn't an industry yet. I felt abandoned, alone, and like a mistake someone was hiding. I heard the caregiver talking about me once. It sounded like no one wanted me.

I vaguely remember seeing an older sister, but I don't recall my mother's visits. She sent money to the family that cared for me. I called the caregiver Aunt Frye. There were other children and grandchildren in a small apartment, living with her as well.

Aunt Frye had a daughter who dated and had men stay over. I'm not sure how long I lived there, but my guess is at least two years. These years embedded trust issues that professional counseling could never penetrate. My relationship with God would be flawed for the next thirty-five years.

Aunt Frye showed me I wasn't wanted emotionally and physically. She told me verbally, and while she scolded me, she reminded me that she was all I had. My older sister told me I lived with them from the age of two until I was four years old. Most of my developmental years were spent believing I was unloved.

Aunt Frye made me wash dishes with a bar of Ivory soap and spanked me if they weren't perfectly clean. She washed my hair with the same bar of soap and put some smelly black pomade on my hair. It stank! I don't ever remember receiving a tub bath or affection while living there. I just remember being bathed in the same sink I washed the dirty dishes in. Maybe there is another reason I don't remember the tub.

I remember playing in the park across the street. I remember kids taunting me about not having a mother or being wanted. I remember sitting on the stoop steps in the East Bronx, wishing, pleading, and hoping my mother would show up and take me away. I fantasized about it in simple ways, just her walking down the street.

I remember wanting to figure out how I could impress my mother into wanting me. What could I do? Would this childhood desire be a foundation of gaining love from others in my future? Yes.

There was no God or church in my life at the time. Aunt Frye threatened me, telling me to stop crying for my mother and complaining because who knows where I would be sent next. I realized I had to accept the reality of whatever happened in that house. I felt it was my fault.

Aunt Frye had at least three kids living with her: her daughter who later had kids, her daughter's boyfriend, and an old man in a back room of the house. I don't remember if this was her father, brother, or husband. This scary man stayed in that back room all day and all night. Even his food was brought to him in that room.

Secrets & Shame

Aunt Frye told me to take a plate of food to the scary man in the back room. I wanted to leave it by the door, but she insisted I take it into the room. I tried to tell her I was scared. She threatened me with a beating if I didn't take the plate in.

I headed to the back room, trying not to spill or drop the big plate in my little hands. I remember wishing someone else were there to give the plate to. The hallway, which was never well lit, was dark and the wood creaky. I barely opened the door to tell the scary man I would leave the plate at the door.

He insisted I bring the plate closer and put it down. I remember him patting the bed for me to jump up and sit on. I tried to say I had to go. He got up and the door closed behind me. The lights went dim. I remember being on the bed, and the memory is gone.

I vaguely remember Aunt Frye telling me I could never tell anyone what happened. She said I would be sent away if I did. I remember sitting on the steps crying for my mother, sister, or anybody. I remember wishing somebody would come for me, rescue me, or care for me. Aunt Frye had me take the food to the scary man other times, too.

According to the psychologist, my memories of what happened in that room were so painful my mind erased them. I have been told the mind protects itself and creates an escape. But for the next 35 years, whenever I would see or hear stories of rape, I would experience a connectivity I didn't understand. I'd always wondered why I felt so strongly about the matter.

Battle Zone

1. Define shame in your own words.

_____

_____

_____

_____

_____

2. Have you ever kept a secret out of fear?

_____

_____

_____

_____

_____

3. Describe a time when you felt unprotected
   as a child.

_____

_____

_____

_____

4. Describe a time when you needed your
   mother or father and they
   were unavailable to you.

_____

_____

_____

_____

Run Don't Look Back

At age five, I went to live with my grandmother in the Bronx. She showed me love for the first time and prayed with me three times a day. She cooked three meals a day, and we had tea and cookies as snacks twice a day because my grandmother was Bahamian, which was a British Commonwealth. We also listened to a radio show at bedtime called "Unshackled."

I was happy living with my grandmother, but something happened to me during that time, too, something I'd hoped to keep secret forever. I delayed writing this book because I always knew neither my mother nor my grandmother could be told.

My grandmother would have been devastated. Her joy and happiness were the most important things to me, and I never wanted my mother to blame herself for what happened to me. I had forgiven her a long time ago. After reviewing her life and struggles, and with God's help, I knew who was to blame.

Angelo was a boy in the neighborhood who was a little older than me, but he always played with me anyway. He asked my grandmother if he could marry me. He told his older brothers and everyone I would be his wife one day. He always pushed me on a bike and taught me to climb.

One day, I was by myself playing, or maybe waiting for a friend to come outside and play. I was on the sidewalk when a man snatched me up and dragged me down the long back alley stairs that led behind my grandmother's six-story apartment building. I tried to yell, but he had his hand over my mouth and threatened to kill me if I didn't keep quiet.

He was huge and strong. There were so many stairs, for they went behind two sets of buildings. My grandmother's window was in the back of the first landing. I tried to call for her, but my mouth was covered.

He carried me behind all the buildings. There was so much trash because people threw junk out their windows. He carried me deep in the back and dropped me on the ground. I couldn't run past him. He said he would kill me. I didn't care. I told him to let me go. I screamed and yelled.

He screamed, "Shut up!"

I refused. I told him, "Kill me. It won't matter."

He responded, "I see you with your little boyfriend playing." He asked, "What did you do with the boy?" I was confused by his question. He said, "Nobody loves or cares for you. You don't have a father. You know what happens to little girls who don't have a father?"

He saw I was listening to him. He continued, "Anybody can do whatever they want because you are not protected. No one loves you."

I told him I didn't care, and I was going. He realized I didn't care about myself, and then said, "I will kill your grandmother."

I remember feeling weak, going limp, and falling to the ground in a squat position. My grandmother was the most important person to me. My grandmother believed in God. My grandmother was holy. I couldn't let anything happen to her. I wasn't important, but my grandmother was Godly.

As I looked at the man, I said, "Kill me. Please don't hurt my grandmother."

He replied, "If you do what I say, I won't hurt your grandmother."

I sat there on the dirty concrete, a soiled mattress and garbage nearby. I heard his words, "Your father doesn't love you, nobody loves you, I will kill your grandmother," repeating in my mind. I wondered why I was even born.

I looked up and the man was opening his belt, pulling his pants down. I saw this thing come out of his pants. I couldn't even imagine what he would do with it. Somehow, he wanted me to do something with it. I couldn't imagine where this could go. I tried to think how something so big could possibly have anything to do with me.

He continued saying, "Your father left you unprotected." He was relishing that he had silenced me with the threat. I would do anything to save my grandmother. She was the only person I had ever known who kind to me was. I thought maybe it would be best for me to be gone. Maybe if he killed me, I wouldn't be a burden any longer.

As he was pulling his pants down further, a bright light shone behind him, a beautiful light and a being very tall compared to me on the ground and the man standing. It had wings or feathers or something that opened wide. It sparkled like a diamond. I wasn't seeing with my eyes but my mind. The man didn't see or sense it there. I can't remember if it was standing or floating. I was fixated on it.

The angel spoke to me. "I want you to run, Lisa."

"No," I answered, "my grandmother will be harmed, and nobody loves or cares for me. I must stay."

"I promise you, your grandmother won't be harmed."

I told the angel the man was bigger than me and I couldn't outrun him.

The angel said, "His pants are near his ankles, and he will be delayed chasing you if you run now." I hesitated. The angel said, "When you run, Lisa, don't look back no matter what. Keep running, and don't look back!"

I got up and ran. I heard the man say, "Get back here!" I could hear him struggling with his pants. I ran as fast as I could. I had about two hundred or more steps to run up to get to the street. I heard him running behind me.

I heard the angel's presence telling me not to look back. I started to hear the man behind me, getting closer and closer. He was skipping steps. I heard, "Run, Lisa." I knew I was about to be caught. I could sense the man reaching out to grab me when I felt a surge, a force that landed me on the sidewalk. I continued to run.

He yelled behind me, "I will get you!" He warned me he'd better not see me alone on the block playing outside. He also said, "I'll kill your grandmother."

When I got upstairs, I didn't tell my grandmother. I remembered how Aunt Frye always said, "If you are trouble, they will send you away." I loved living with my grandmother. I didn't want to be sent somewhere else.

I asked my grandmother what happens when a man takes and hurts a little girl. She asked why I'd asked. I told her I heard people talking.

My grandmother said, "If that happens to a girl, her life is ruined. She might never marry, and it would bring shame to her parents and family."

I knew from my grandmother's response shame was a bad thing. I knew I could never tell her. I never wanted her to think I was a bad girl. I didn't understand what I had done to deserve the fear I had. I remembered the man's words; it was because I didn't have a father. He said this happens to little girls without a dad. Those words haunted me.

Over the next few days, I got in trouble numerous times. My grandmother sent me to the store to get milk or bread. I would sneak outside, looking for the man lurking about. He stayed on the corner by the convenience store. There was no way to get to the store without him seeing me, so I traveled the opposite way and went four blocks or more, so I could enter the store from the other side.

When it was time to leave, I had to go back that way as well. The trip to the store usually only took five minutes from my grandmother's, but it took me an hour to get back and I got scolded for not coming straight home.

When my grandmother and I went to church together, I saw the man start walking toward us. My grandmother was talking, and I knew he wouldn't grab me with my grandmother there. When my grandmother and I would return from church at night, I would watch to make sure no one was following us. I was filled with fear and anxiety as we walked in the night.

Weeks later, I was walking home from school with friends, and I saw the police parked in front of my building. As I entered the lobby, I saw my grandmother on the ground, upset, with police officers around her. When she saw me she cried out, "Lisa?" She held me, crying and saying she was glad I was safe.

I asked, "What happened?"

The police stated someone with a knife tried to rob her and steal her purse. They said that my grandmother snatched the bag back and the robber threatened to kill her. My grandmother said, "I'm glad you are safe," and held me tightly with shaking hands. I had never seen her so shaken. She said, "He tried to kill me."

I knew it was because of me.

My grandmother was still shaking when we got into the apartment. I realized the man was making good on his promise. I tried to comfort my grandmother. The next day we went to the store to buy a cassette player. My grandmother, realizing she had almost died, wanted to record us singing together on the cassette player. As we sang "I Promise Him," I saw how devastated she was.

I heard an unkind voice telling me, "You did this by running. Your grandmother was attacked because of *you*." I heard the voice state, "He will come back and kill her next time because of *you*."

I realized what I needed to do.

As we recorded, I was glad my grandmother would have my voice to remember me by on tape. After we'd made three tapes and my grandmother got busy making dinner, I thought to myself, *this is my chance*. The only way to stop the man was to remove myself. I believed, or the voice in my head stated, that if I killed myself, he wouldn't harm my grandmother.

I went into the bedroom and decided that jumping out the window would be the quickest and fastest way to end my life. My grandmother was singing a church hymn in the kitchen as she always did. I opened the windows wide as I could. I climbed up and stood on the windowsill. A neighbor in an apartment two floors down started pounding her window, saying, "Get down!" as she tried to get her window opened. If she did and yelled, she would alert my grandmother.

I knew I had to jump right then. With no thought for myself, I turned to jump. Suddenly, the brightest light, the colorful angel, was there in front of me, outside the window. He asked what I was doing. I told him he'd promised my grandmother would not get hurt, but she had been attacked.

"This man will kill her if I don't die. I must protect my grandmother, and no one wants me or will miss me." I continued, "I must do this."

The angel said, "Do you know how devastated your grandmother would be if you were to jump? She will blame herself. She will think it was her fault."

"But it's *not* her fault," I said.

The angel asked me to go back inside for a moment. I went back in and said, "I don't want her to blame herself. My parents will be happy."

"Your grandmother loves you. She will never forgive herself." I started to cry because I didn't know what to do. "I can't ruin her life, but if I stay, the man will harm her."

The angel said, "What if I promise that neither you nor your grandmother will be harmed?"

"I'm a child, and men are too big for me to fight. I don't like them, and nobody watches over me."

The angel replied, "That's not true. One day, you will manage many men, and they will fear you. You will be successful, smart, and special. This memory I can take away until later."

I asked, "Why would you do this for me? Why do you care? Why did I come to such a place?"

"We have a lot in common."

I looked at him through my mind, so I can't remember the details of his face. He beamed too brightly for me to see features. I felt him and heard him in my mind. "I, too, was willing to die for the ones I loved." He told me, "It takes a special person to lay down her life for another. Because of what you were willing to do, I am going to give you something special. I want you to remember no one will ever hurt you or your grandmother. Neither she nor you will be in danger."

He continued, "When you cry, I feel every tear." He told me to remember what he'd said and that it would all make sense one day.

Thirty-five years later, the Lord told me he'd had to respond when the enemy said, "Your father doesn't love you; your father left you unprotected." The Lord said, "You thought the man was talking about your earthly father, but the accusation was against Me."

The Lord told me all the things I would do in the future. I said, "No way! How is that possible?"

The angel said, "You are beautiful. You won't remember this until many years from now. I am giving you confidence to do all things."

I sensed that he would be watching me. It never occurred to me to ask him who he was, although I knew who he was, if that makes sense. I knew we were connected. I was too young to have the mind to capture the vastness of the moment nor was I supposed to at the time.

The next thing I knew, my grandmother called for me. "Lee Lee, come for dinner." She played a baby game with me because I didn't like to eat much. She fed me and told me she would have never made it through the last few weeks without me. She promised me that my Grandpa, whom I had never met, loved me and would visit me one day.

I asked, "Does he know about me?"

"I'm sure he does, and he wants you to eat your food. You are the baby."

"Really?"

She assured me I would always be the baby to her. My grandmother called me that until she died in her sleep at age ninety-five. My grandfather did come to visit me a few years later. We had a very special time together as a family.

My Defender

In the following days, I saw Angelo, who asked why he hadn't seen me. I told him what the man on the corner did to me. Thinking back now, I freely told him. Angelo was upset. He was about ten years old. He called to his brother upstairs, who called back.

Angelo took me by the hand and led me up to his apartment, saying, "I want you to tell my brother what happened."

I said, "No, I don't want anything to do with that guy."

"My brother will handle him."

Once inside their apartment, I told him what the man did to me behind the building. His brother said, "What?! Let's go!" Outside, as I stood some ways off, Angelo's brother approached the guy on the corner. He told him what he'd heard, and the man started to deny it.

Angelo's older brother said, "Why would she lie? She is only a small little girl." By now all the boys and men on the corner heard Angelo's brother, who then took the man by the neck, pushed him up against the wall and told him, "If you ever go near her again, I'll kill you. Don't even look at her if she's outside." He told every guy on the corner, "If you see him look her direction, tell me and I will bust him up."

Turned out the man was a nineteen or twenty years-old. He was old and huge compared to me. Angelo's brother asked me, "Lisa, do you want me to beat his ass?"

I said, "I don't want him to ever come near me or look at my grandmother ever again."

Angelo's brother told the guy, "This is my little sister. You look at her again, you are dead." The man tried to make excuses but then shut up.

Angelo chimed in by saying, "Yeah, punk, don't look at me, either." I remember Angelo turning to me and saying, "I told you I would protect you."

I remembered someone else had told me that, but I couldn't remember who.

Angelo was bold enough to tell my Grandma Cooper again that he would marry me one day. My grandmother laughed at him because he was so serious. She waved at him like, "You're so cute."

As we walked away Angelo said, "It will happen, Lisa."

I was happy it was all over and felt safe. My grandmother looked happy and was laughing. She would tell that joke for decades to come.

Battle Zone

1. Have you ever felt your life threatened?

_____

_____

_____

_____

2. Have you hidden the truth to spare
someone's feelings or life?

_____

_____

_____

_____

3. Have you ever been in the presence of
angels or the Lord?

_____

_____

_____

_____

_____

4. Describe a time when your life was spared
from harm.

_____

_____

_____

_____

5. Describe what it is like to live with the secret of shame in your life.

_____

_____

_____

_____

6. Has shame impacted the people you date, married, or worked with?

_____

_____

_____

_____

7. Have you experienced shame within your family, school, workplace, dating, church, or somewhere else?

_____

_____

_____

_____

8. How have you felt when somebody stood up for you?

_____

_____

_____

_____

9. How did you get out of the situation?

_____

_____

_____

_____

_____

Hospital

I was in the ER for over an hour with memories of my life swirling in my head. I began to feel worse and told the nurse, who hadn't checked my vitals or anything. She looked at me and said, "You look flushed," and took my blood pressure. The nurse then said, "Oh my," and went on full alert.

My blood pressure was in the two hundred. They quickly wheeled me off to do a CAT scan, during which the doctors asked what I had been doing immediately prior. I told them I had been sitting in the lobby for an hour, and prior to that, I'd been with a psychologist, trying to recover a painful childhood memory. I mentioned I was also in the middle of moving, buying a home, and a company reorganization.

The doctor said, "No more trying to remember painful childhood memories," and asked if I had high blood pressure.

"No, but it runs in my family."

The CAT scan test came back normal. I was told to relax and do no more memory pulling. I went home.

The memories continued flashing and became clearer. Things I had always sensed were being confirmed. Again, I saw myself praying at age twenty-six, promising God that when I became a Vice President in corporate America, I would give my life to him. I had made a promise, and God was ready to collect.

While I rested and slept, the gaps in what had happened at my grandmother's house as a child became clearer. Jesus' words had been fulfilled about men, His protection, my confidence and boldness, and letting go of my grandmother. The memories were causing a physical reaction that was a war the devil had been waging against me since my childhood.

Within two weeks after my hospital visit, I was driving when I felt my chest pounding again. I drove to the ER closest to me, and I was given another CAT scan. Based on the scan results, the doctors believed that I had suffered a stroke during my prior visit to the ER. The medicine I was given didn't bring my blood pressure down. The doctor was worried. He had me moved to intensive care. He was concerned I would go into cardiac arrest.

They called my ex-husband, Andre, who came to the hospital. The doctor told him, "She has a strong heart, but I can't give her any more medicine and her blood pressure is still rising."

Andre sat next to me on the bed as we watched my pressure continue to climb. I'll never forget his words. "Lisa, I know you, and you are stronger than this. Bring your pressure down. You can do it."

The doctor told the staff to be ready.

I looked at Andre and said, "I want to see the boys. Please bring them."

Seeing what I had suffered as a child brought back the pain, fear, the abandonment, the running, and the being chased. I didn't realize until then that I had been running from the truth of feeling unwanted, alone, abused, and mistreated; of being four years old and sitting on the stoop, looking for my mother. I remembered the broken heart and deception I'd suffered as a young woman. I started remembering I'd wanted to die a long time ago.

While I was in that hospital bed, surrounded with memories, I began to feel tired of fighting for everything in life. The devil had me on the ropes. He started speaking in my ear, and I was listening. He said, "Your insurance policy is high. Your kids will be rich if you are dead. Your children will be better off without you anyway. You wanted to die before so let it happen."

Meanwhile, Andre was in the background saying,

"Fight, Lisa."

I faded into all that had happened to me in my past. I believed I was a mistake. All the bad things happened because I was a mistake. My whole life I had been trying to prove I was not a mistake. If I had been planned and wanted, my life would not have had so many hurdles and near-death escapes.

How many times had I or my family almost been killed? Why was life such a battle for me? The devil had many answers as I traveled back in time, recalling the tragedies while I was in the ICU.

When my three sons arrived to join their dad, I knew that Andre was seriously worried about me. The doctor told him they were trying to manage how the stroke would affect me. The doctor was convinced my heart couldn't take this amount of pressure for much longer.

Andre was my light in that hospital room. He said, "Lisa, you can do this. Make your blood pressure go down. We need you."

I held each of my sons; two would be high school sophomores, and the other was in kindergarten. I said, "I love you." I wish I could say what happened in that room. I remember closing my eyes and the memories continuing as my pressure stayed high.

The nurse said, "It's up to her now. We can do no more."

I was past Man's ability to save me. The Lisa that God loved and had always given the strength to fight had stopped fighting.

I said, "It's your choice, God. I'm tired of fighting."\

As I held my son's hand, I asked Andre to take them back to the hotel. If I was going to stroke or worse, I didn't want them there to witness it.

My blood pressure stayed over two hundred and twenty. I wondered, *what am I going to do in Atlanta that the enemy needs to take me out now?* I knew the devil had tried to destroy me my whole life. I was in a war, but I knew that God was fighting for me.

Because He was, I had some realizations and revelations that helped me fight back.

TAKE-BACK STRATEGIES

Understanding Shame

I realized that shame kept me trapped in a box for a long time. Shame is a secret you share with no one because you believe they may look at you or treat you differently. Every person has something in their life they have felt shameful about.

The devil keeps you locked in a box alone, believing only you have had this horrible experience and nobody would ever understand your problem; it is unique to you and makes you look bad. You can't share this pain, or everyone will spread the word.

My mom used to say, "You can't trust anybody with your secrets." Yet secrets and burdens of the heart and mind do kill people. How long can women stuff their pain within? You run out of space inside yourself, and then your pain flows all over everyone else. Every organ in your body holds emotional and physical pain. But if you free yourself of condemnation, you might stop the disease of high blood pressure, diabetes, obesity, depression, heartache, and anxiety.

What is shame? Merriam-Webster defines it as a feeling of guilt, regret, sadness you have because you know you have done something wrong; the ability to feel guilt, regret, or embarrassment; and dishonor or disgrace.

Please circle any of the below that have made you feel shame. Add to the list if needed.

- Multiple fathers of children
- Poverty
- Broken heartedness
- Loneliness

- Singleness
- Abortion
- Unwed pregnancy
- Domestic abuse
- Date rape
- Incest
- Sex with a married man
- Lesbian relationship
- Molestation
- Addictions
- Criminal offender

What have you used to relieve the pain of shame? Drugs, alcohol, money, counseling, work, men, or something else? Has it worked?

When you reflect on the first time you felt shame, you may find the situation was not something you could have changed or affected. For example: alcoholic parents, incest, rape, molestation – these were things done to you. You are not the bad girl or the reason these individuals committed a crime *against* you.

What I've Learned

We all have done or had an experience that we want to keep hidden, or we regret or feel embarrassed about. Too many of us have experienced being dishonored by others at a young age and as adults. We live feeling alone or trapped, bottled up with emotions and pain too difficult to deal with.

These emotions lead to a battlefield where we are unprepared and unarmed to defend ourselves. This is where the devil is waiting with reinforcements to help you believe what's happened to you was your fault and you deserve everything bad that happens from then on. That is all garbage from the pit of Hell, I tell you!

In the hospital, I laid there remembering all the battles. I knew all the near deaths were to prevent me from coming to this place. What would happen here in this city that would be worth me losing my life over?

Through prayer and fresh eyes, pick three events you deem shameful from your youth that came to mind while reading this chapter. When did it first begin? Think of the very first memory of shame. Can you see a chain of events link? Was the first link a parent or relative? Did you judge them?

The first thing you must identify is: The lies

Second thing: What's the truth about you in God's word?

The third thing is to pray and ask Jesus for revelation and healing over the situation.

People to forgive will come to mind. Start keeping a *Forgiveness List* for future chapters.

Warrior Woman Prayer

Let's talk briefly about praying. God knows your heart and the honesty of your words. Don't try to pray like somebody else or quote scriptures to impress God or people. The Lord likes honest, simple, and humble prayers. Praying is talking to and waiting upon the Lord Jesus. He does talk back so be ready to hear Him.

Here is a sample prayer to remove shame from your life:

Jesus, I thank you for this day and opportunity to break shame off my life. I repent for believing the lies _____, _____, and _____.

I choose today to believe your word that states, I am _____, _____, and _____.

I forgive all those who have hurt and wrongfully abused and shamed me before my Lord. Into your hands I give them to you. I accept you as My Lord, My Savior, My Judge, and My King.

HOW DO YOU RELEASE SHAME FROM YOUR LIFE?

What does God's word say about shame?

1 John 1:9
"If we confess our sins, He is faithful and just and will forgive us our sins and purify us from all unrighteousness."

Romans 10:11
"As scripture says, anyone who believes in Him will never be put to shame."

Shame brought on from what others have done to you is healed through your forgiveness toward those who've violated you. Forgiveness does not release the person from legal or damage responsibility. It releases you from carrying and keeping alive the person, pain, and memory of what they did to you.

For me, forgiveness was a process. Yes, I said the words, but I also noticed when I forgave someone, neither their name nor the circumstance caused a reaction from me physically or emotionally. What I learned through experience is when you pray and release the person into God's hands, the Lord will sometimes let you see the results of your prayer. What's empowering and humbling is to release the person into God's hands and judgment.

If you feel shame from your own actions, then prayer and repentance is needed.

Here are what the two different prayers might look like:

Lord, I pray to forgive _____ *&* _____ *for the shame they have attached to my identity. Lord, I release to you all the lies, feelings, and emotions attached to the harm they have done such as:* _____, _____, _____. *I ask forgiveness for believing the lies that their actions were my fault. Father, I lay down my judgment and place them in the hands of their creator. I trust your love and righteousness in Jesus Name.*

Lord, I repent for engaging in actions that led to my shame. I was wrong when I _____, _____, _____. *Father, I ask for your forgiveness. I pray to learn and grow to be a faithful daughter of the highest God.*

SPEAK OUT LOUD

Take-Back Statements

State them out loud:

- I am worthy.
- I am respectful.
- I am pure.
- I am holy before God.
- I am a new creature.
- I am free from shame.
- I am no longer a victim.
- I have a future.
- I have hope.
- I have joy.

Add what the Lord puts in your heart. Fill your soul with truth. You will do this every time anyone or something tries to remind you of shame. Be direct, be clear, and speak your truth and worth. Don't give your worth away again.

Chapter Two

Regret

Philippians 3:13

"Brothers and sisters, I do not consider myself yet to have taken hold of it. But one thing I do: Forgetting what is behind and straining toward what is ahead, I press on toward the goal to win the prize for which God has called me heavenward in Christ Jesus."

Matthew 6:19-20

"Do not store up for yourselves treasures on earth, where moth and vermin destroy and where thieves break in and steal. But store up for yourselves treasures in heaven, where moths and vermin do not destroy, and where thieves do not break in and steal."

Before we begin, list five things you regret about your life right now:

_____

_____

_____

_____

_____

Before Atlanta, I was living in Dallas, Texas, as an executive with a great company. I had gone on a business trip to Maui, Hawaii, and decided to stay for a week after my meetings. While I was there, I purchased two beachfront units to vacation in and have a place for my sons. While I was climbing a mountain to see the sunrise early one morning, I realized I was where I'd dreamt to be at this point in my life.

As I stood there feeling hopeful and impressed by the wonder of God's hand, the Lord asked me a question. He asked me, "Was it worth it?" I was startled at the question because I was in a great mood. The Lord was asking me if all that I had been through in corporate America was worth where I was standing right now. Was all the disappointment, depression, stress, lack of sleep, worry, anxiety, racism, sexual harassment, belittling worth what I could buy today? The Lord said, "You can buy and do what you want now, but was it worth it?"

As I looked at the sunrise that day, I realized I had turned down several good offers of marriage for my career and the fear of failure twice. I thought about why I didn't change careers or start a business after the racism. I thought about the time away from my kids and my son telling me he would rather have less toys and a smaller house if I didn't travel.

As the sun began to rise, I stood on that mountain. I had it all according to my plan ... didn't I? I had to prove it to myself that I could be as smart as a white male in business. What was driving me to reach that mountain top? That day, I realized the pain wasn't worth the price I'd paid for it.

A couple of months later, I had decided to buy a lakefront property in Texas that backed up to a natural preserve that could never be built on. The only access to the preserve would be on my property or by boat, which would be great. I thought, *I will put down roots and build a place to bring my sons on the weekends.* I had decided to not pursue advancement outside my company.

Two weeks after I put the down payment on the best lot with a boat dock, a recruiter called about a Group Vice President position, one with eleven Vice Presidents reporting to me. The position would triple my pay, have executive benefits, stock, and more. The position would be a huge promotion. When I mentioned it to friends, they told me I would be crazy to turn it down.

I knew something didn't feel right. My ex-husband told me he'd never seen me back down from an opportunity, but I told him something just wasn't right. He asked if I was nervous because he had never seen me nervous about a job. I told him it was something else that I couldn't figure out.

The position would require I move to St. Louis, and I had just planned to build on the lake. I got my deposit back on the property, and when all my household goods were packed and on two eighteen-wheeler trucks outside my house, I felt that feeling again like I should not take the position. I told my ex-husband I felt as though I was being tricked. I told him something was wrong, and I should have them unpack my things.

I did regret not trusting my instincts because something was wrong as you read earlier. Even in the regret of the corporate move, God had a plan to get me to Atlanta with a future of being an author that would lead women to seek Christ.

So many times, we stay in the mindset of what we've done wrong instead of seeking God for guidance as to where we should go. My healing, my relationship with God, my ministry, and now this book was birthed out of a painful situation I regret. Let God show you a path out of regret to a promise of unimaginable experiences. I would have never experienced all the miracles, healings, and lives changed if I hadn't experienced the disappointment and regret in my past.

Let your regrets propel you to a powerful plan from God.

Regret is the younger sibling of shame. Regret, Bitterness, Anger, and Shame have the same dad, the Father of Lies.

Women & Regret

Women are at a higher risk of poverty in America. Among industrialized nations, the U.S. has the largest number of homeless women and children. According to the U.S. Census Bureau data:

- Women are 35% more likely than men to live in poverty.
- One in eight women lived in poverty in 2016.
- One in three single mothers lived in poverty in 2015.

Of the nation's fourteen and a half million poor children, more than half live in families headed by a woman.

Why are they more likely to suffer in poverty?

Women are more likely to be undercompensated, overrepresented in low wage jobs, and more likely to do unpaid caregiving work (*quote from your dream blog*, "5 Problems Still Facing Women In 2017").

A woman who hasn't graduated college makes 67% less than a woman who has a bachelor's degree. Single moms struggle to attend college due to childcare and housing, plus possibly the lack of consistent child support.

- Each year, forty-seven million American women experience physical violence by a partner.
- Domestic violence costs the economy between ten and sixty-seven billion dollars each year.
- One in five college women has been sexually assaulted while attending college
- Physical abuse of women starts early in life; 76% of teens have experienced some form of dating violence.
- 67% of single moms do not attend church, according to CBN.

I was shocked to see such a high percent of single moms that don't attend church. I expected a much lower percentage. With the information above, is it shocking to see the struggles women are having? Without God, you will lose and be unprotected in a cruel world.

I wanted to know: what are the top five things women regret? I am going to look at two sources. The first is a survey done in the U.K. of one thousand women, aged twenty-five to thirty-nine, carried out by Diet Coke as part of their "Regret Nothing" campaign. The second comes from *Inc. Magazine*.

Women's Biggest Regrets:

1. Not trying hard enough in school
2. Not losing weight on a diet
3. Choosing the wrong career path

4. Not getting on the property ladder

5. Spending a night with someone I shouldn't have

Top 5 Regrets of People Dying:

- I wish that I had let myself be happier.

- I wish I hadn't worked so hard.

- I wish I'd had the courage to live a life true to myself, not the life others expected of me.

- I wish I'd had the courage to express my feelings.

- I wish I had stayed in touch with my friends.

Can you relate to any of the above regrets? You are about to be the smartest woman alive. Both above groups missed understanding that if they had chosen to have God in their lives, they would have made better decisions. Even those dying missed the knowledge of Christ in their lives.

Regret leads to condemnation, which keeps you amongst the family members of shame. Condemnation means: a statement or expression of very strong and definite criticism or disapproval. In layman terms, you prosecute and render judgment upon yourself.

In ministry, I hear women state they are stupid, dumb, fat, ugly, and more because of circumstances they regret.

Let's look at the "re-" prefix, meaning to indicate repetition or meaning backward, to indicate withdrawal. My question to you is, how many times do you want to repeat or look back at a problem that's done and over? When you regret, you withdraw from your future to dwell backward. You need to be present in your future, or it will be stolen from you.

Does that sound like a place you should be? Living in regret is sad. Regret leads to depression. What a cycle to find yourself in. Now you are going backward while being pushed lower. Stop and think of that visually. You must stop the cycle. Let's not depend on a man or many men, drugs or alcohol to keep us stable. Depend on Jesus. When you know the right thing to do and it appears hard, don't let your emotions lead to the wrong outcome which results in more regret.

Battle Zone

1. In your list of regrets from the beginning of the chapter, was God in the plan?

_____

_____

_____

_____

2. Do you work for earthly needs or excesses?

_____

_____

_____

_____

3. Are you trying to measure yourself or your success against a certain group of people, family?

_____

_____

_____

_____

4. Is people-pleasing leading to regret? Explain how.

_____

_____

_____

_____

5. Are you in the career you desire?

_____
_____
_____
_____
_____

6. Do you spend time with close friends?

_____
_____
_____
_____

7. What can you do to reverse your list
    of regrets into progress?

_____
_____
_____
_____

Prayer to Get Rid of Regret

Father, please break the cycle of shame off my life. Lord, I repent for believing in the spirit of "I." You have my beginning and my end already planned. I shall be set free from regret and all links to the spirit of shame. Your word bears my identity. Amen.

Jealousy

Jealousy is related to regret but a first cousin of hate and anger. Regret keeps you in a state of being left behind in self-loathing or self-hate. Jealousy makes you hate others that you believe have it made or are living your dream life.

Women forget there are no perfect people. Women, no matter who they are, will find something they don't like about themselves and complain about it to someone. If you gave woman a million dollars, she would still say, "I'm rich but look at my thighs!" Really!

Jealousy is a habit woman practice early by watching and looking for those who are prettier, have a good looking wealthy man, longer hair, lighter skin color, or better body to envy. Over time, that envy slides easily into jealousy. What's funny about women is, if you stop to think about it, every woman you envy has a woman that they envy, and the cycle goes on and on.

Social Media

Let's take social media. People who spend all their time sharing hot pics or trying to show you they are having a great time are not having a great time. Great pics do not equal a good life. People use social media to fake it. They need people to think they have it all. If they were that happy, they wouldn't be on social media for hours at a time.

How sad is it that women are waiting to see how many "likes" they get? Now we have added another dynamic to jealousy which is at the heart of it for women: who is more popular or getting the attention?

Top Jealousy Pics for Women

- Boyfriend, husband (rich, of course)
- Perfect hair
- Great body (boob job)
- Lips, eyes
- Career
- Attention
- The girl who has all the above
- Money
- Vacation

If a woman has all the above, when would she have time to spend hours on social media? Jealousy can lead to hate and murder. Ugghhh!

What is the root cause of jealousy? Lack of identity. Women have the reputation of harboring jealousy because the world decides which type of woman is beautiful.

Is it the skinny girl, big girls, voluptuous, or big lipped? If you are not the girl type being written about, talked about, or have the unlimited funds to have plastic surgery every time a new look is applauded, you may have some jealousy lurking around.

How Can You Tell If Someone Has Jealousy Issues?

- I learned they put others down constantly.
- Critically judging themselves against others constantly.
- Envy others' lives on social media.
- Try to dress or look like others.
- Talk about others excessively.

Imagine you are God, listening to someone like you being critical of who they are and unhappy with the woman You created. You are a one-of-a-kind woman in the whole world, yet you spend your days complaining about the rare, unique woman you are. Society teaches women to be a copy of their ideal woman of the hour. God is a creative God, and He made each of us unique and purposeful with different talents.

How dare we complain each day about what we look like when we don't even know what beautiful is, or our full capability as believers in Jesus?

Christian Jealousy

Christian women are no better than women in the world, except their lists may be longer. Christian women add all the spiritual gifts and talents to the list. Example: "I wish I could pray like that. I wish I had her faith." Many people sound like they pray well in public, but unless you know their lifestyles, their prayers may never reach Jesus' ears.

We Christian women spend too much time evaluating what we look like on the outside when our insides look like a trash compactor, everything shoved and stuffed underneath the clothes. Don't be jealous of another woman. Be brave and release the woman God called you to be.

Family Jealousy

I am sure this is a taboo subject for many families to discuss, but it is too prevalent to ignore. During my healing sessions I had to forgive my parents and siblings for my perceived feelings of abandonment, shame, unworthiness, jealousy, and more.

Being the youngest of six children, it was rare or nonexistent to receive a compliment or an encouraging word about anything I ever accomplished or achieved in my business, career, or personal life. I remember criticism or side jokes. My mother and father (especially) were complimentary. I never had siblings cheering me on to success during difficult times of struggles.

I never had the hug or shoulder to cry on.

Twenty years ago, I tried to address the problem at a family reunion and to start the healing process with a professional counselor waiting for the green light to join. But my siblings were still in the blame mode. Jealousy and unforgiveness are siblings of the root of hate and murder in the spirit realm. If you can't break through on unforgiveness, bitterness, and pride with love, it's hard to reach the root of jealousy.

When we are over 35 years old, we should have matured past blaming others for our behaviors, hurt, pain, and shame. The spirit of jealousy never wants to listen or hear another perspective. Have you ever tried to explain your hurt to someone and they were too busy thinking of countering your words instead of listening and comprehending what you are sharing? Hate has no ears to hear. They may also throw it back to you as if it is your fault they hurt you? Sad. Listening is a skill many do not possess.

My siblings are much older than me, so when I was 14 years old, all except one of my siblings were in their twenties and thirties. During healing, I had to forgive and not hold on to what somebody should have done. I let go of feelings of abandonment when I was young, never hearing "I love you" from a sibling, experiencing a lack of support when my father was sick and died, gaining full custody of my father from his wife at age twenty-one in court alone, times of choosing college and going by myself to evaluate, my divorce, my lawsuit against a major corporation, as a single parent, and in financial crisis.

I had a foundation of woundedness which allowed me to make a life for myself and my children. I had a different idea of family. I had to forgive.

This is something I also tackled in forgiveness and ancestral patterns. As the youngest with a huge age gap, I expected more than they can give. Maybe it's due to having different fathers and the age gap. Whatever the cause, we must pray to God for all our cares whether it's jealousy or forgiveness. You could be thinking maybe it's selfishness or inconsideration. Those are manifestations of a root.

What's the root? Hate. The Lord shared these thoughts as well:

- The person manifesting jealousy against or toward you suffers from self-hate first.
- Forgive them because it's not about you anyway. They are hurt themselves.
- Pray they gain the ability to hear.
- As they begin to heal, they can see, hear, and speak words of love and encouragement toward others.

Scripture
1 John 2:9-11
"Anyone who claims to be in the light but hates a brother or sister is still in the darkness. Anyone who loves their brother and sister lives in the light, and there is nothing in them to make them stumble.

Proverbs 10:18
"But anyone who hates a brother or sister is in the darkness and walks around in the darkness. They do not know where they are going, because the darkness has blinded them."

Psalms 36:2
"Whoever conceals hatred with lying lips and spreads slander is a fool."

Proverbs 10:12
"In their own eyes they flatter themselves too much to detect or hate their sin."

"Hatred stirs up conflict, but love covers over all wrongs."

I saw my Dad regularly and was encouraged by him. The siblings closest in age to me didn't have that. There lies a possible reason or cause that I have accepted and forgiven whatever the reason.

BATTLE ZONES

1. What about your family and jealousy

_____
_____
_____

_____

2. Have you ever expressed your feelings
with your siblings or parents

_____
_____
_____

_____

3. Do you have siblings with a different dad
or mom that have led to similar feelings?

_____
_____

_____

4. How has jealousy manifested itself
among your family members?

_____
_____

_____

5. Can you see the root of hate and or
    murder in their lives and yours?

_____

_____

_____

_____

6. Do you praise family members or other
    women on their successes easily?

_____

_____

_____

_____

7. What do you need forgiveness for in
    family jealousy?

_____

_____

_____

Jealousy is the excuse to not fulfill your purpose. Jealousy gives you the excuse that your abilities are limited, and you are less than another woman, so you can't accomplish much. I had a woman who believed her weight and lips were keeping her from getting married. It wasn't her weight or lips. It was her mindset because there are many married women who struggle with their weight.

When you read and gain revelation about the special you that God wants to heal to impact the world, then you will see the best within yourself. I can admire someone, but I choose to embrace and learn all that I can do with my mind, body, and soul.

Battle Zones

1. List the top ten things you love about
    yourself.

_____

_____

_____

_____

2. What's unique about you?

_____

_____

_____

_____

3. Who do you envy and why?

_____

_____

_____

_____

4. List people you are jealous of. If you
    don't list someone, you are being untruthful.

_____

_____

_____

_____

Repent

Father, I apologize for not appreciating all the beauty and uniqueness you knitted in my mother's womb. Lord, forgive me for being jealous of or envying _____, _____, _____, _____, _____.

I shall make it a daily habit of thanking you and displaying my uniqueness in my prayers and in the world. Every day, I shall choose to be grateful for who and what I have, in Jesus' name

Chapter Three

Forgiveness

Mark 11:25-26

"And when you stand praying, if you hold anything against anyone, forgive them, so that your Father in heaven may forgive you your sins."

Matthew 6:15

"But if you do not forgive others their sins, your Father will not forgive your sins."

We all know we should forgive others, but do we? Sometimes our mouths speak the words, which is a good start, but it's not in our hearts. How do you know if you have forgiven? If every time the person's name is mentioned or a similar situation arises you revert to what they did to you, you haven't forgiven. Mark 11:25 says that forgiveness is not a conditional or negotiable thing. God's word is clear about forgiveness.

Forgiveness became easier for me when I activated Matthew 6:15 against those who offended me. If not forgiving someone is going to put me out of alignment with God, I am forgiving them. A warrior doesn't give up her sword to someone trying to attack them in the physical realm. If you don't forgive, you are giving them the sword to your eternal soul. What has someone done to you that would be worth losing your blessings and eternal life? We won't even get into the physical danger to your health by harboring unforgiveness.

Sickness and disease are destroying women who harbor bitterness, anger, and hate. I was shocked at how good I felt when I released forgiveness against those that caused me pain.

The Lord Responds

I will tell you, my experience has been God's payback or judgment is far harsher than mine. Initially, we're upset and want them roughed up a little, but as time goes on and you have let it go, it doesn't mean the person's actions have been forgotten by God. The Lord has let me witness the response of men, companies, managers that I have had a relationship with since I was sixteen years old. You will say, "Is this for everyone?" Yes. I noticed those I seriously cried over. I had to pray for mercy because I saw God's response.

Whether it was personal relationships, family, employers, or managers, the Lord brought me justice. After twenty years, I have received calls or had conversations to apologize and share how their struggle led God to show they needed to apologize to me. When you decide to pay people back or to hold on to anger, it affects you and every interaction you have with others. It's like wearing a big top hat that says, "Hurt, abused victim coming through." Don't let the actions of others make you bear the trauma and destruction for many years to come. You deserve life abundantly.

Solution

Why would you forgive those who have hurt or offended you when you feel they don't deserve your forgiveness?

- First, you are to be Christlike, set apart from the actions so common to others.
- Jesus forgave those who abandoned Him to be crucified. He bore every shame, pain, and disease so you could have a role model to follow.

- You can't be a Christian if your heart and behavior don't reflect who you serve. Easy, they are not losing an ounce of sleep over your unforgiveness.
- Your emotions, health, and time are being wasted.
- You pray for God's justice. *Isaiah, 30:18: "Therefore the LORD longs to be gracious to you, And therefore He waits on high to have compassion on you For the Lord is a God of justice; How blessed are all those who long for Him."*
- Don't let somebody steal your health, emotions, sound mind, joy, and future relationships with unforgiveness.

I recently saw a person I had not seen in over thirty years. They were about ten years older than I was. The person was cruel to me as a child. I didn't flinch or act disgusted. After my husband and I left, I told him who they were and what I remembered.

He was surprised I was so friendly and engaging with the person. It was confirmed in my spirit that it could only be God that allowed me to greet them and their family with a smile and engage them in conversation like there was no past. Forgiveness never holds the past hostage.

This is an example of why God is real to me. I could not have done this in my own strength.

This reaction was the result of the work I did in forgiveness and healing for years. That meeting confirmed my healing. I wasn't the abandoned little girl without an identity. I was a daughter of a King. I had a renewed mind. I had the Holy Spirit.

Most of all, I knew who God called me to be. How do you know you are healed unless you face it? God has given me an opportunity to see the people who have stolen and robbed something from me. I no longer have judgment. I put my trust in God to bring me justice.

I'm not afraid to confront or debate anybody. Their offense was stricken from my memory the same way I want all my sins forgotten by God. It was not hard, nor did it change my usual behavior. When I was leaving, the Holy Spirit brought it to my memory to share just how far I had come in faith and forgiveness in this area. Don't think I have it all worked out, by any means. Every day, I struggle and fight like everybody else. My warfare is grounded in three things: I am human, and the word and prayer are needed often and much.

Testimony

I had an experience with a believer who I dated once. He never told me he was still married. I had no reason to believe he wasn't single. It felt like such a great beginning to a relationship with someone who had the same faith and shared the same social/community interests. It was complicated after I learned the truth. I was left feeling hurt and disillusioned. I was having dreams, or warnings, about the person. I was very disappointed. I knew I had to forgive, and in my woundedness, I began to pray. As I was praying, I heard a voice say, "Tell God to curse his life for hurting you." I felt the struggle of falling for my emotions. I heard the voice again say, "You know if you say it, He will do it."

In that moment, I knew the voice was right; God would do it. I also remembered what the word states in Psalms 55:22, to cast all your cares. I also knew if I prayed for his demise, I would be against God and would fall under judgment. In my tears, I cried forgiveness for the person and for myself. I prayed to never let myself fall prey to wishing them harm.

Two years later as I was leaving church, I bumped into that same person. He didn't look good. God brought his judgment. He stated everything I had shared with him about the choices he'd made had brought a judgment upon his life. He looked at me with sincere eyes and said, "I miss you, and I'm so sorry I hurt you."

I stopped him and said, "The choice has already been made, and we must live with our decisions. I forgave you two years ago." I wished him well and walked away. In that moment, I didn't celebrate that his life was in misery. I thought he was off living a happy life. I thanked God for showing me his response.

I prayed God would restore him with peace, faith, and redemption. You may think I was in a new relationship at the time. No, I was single, happy, and content with my life. I was healed and forgiven by God. I felt covered by God in that moment. You see, God didn't have to ever show me his life. It felt like a checkup. I saw someone in need of a healer, and I prayed.

Years later, I happened upon a social media page and noticed he was on a mission trip, being baptized. I smiled and felt peace in the Lord.

Hard to Forgive

When I struggle with forgiveness, I remember Luke 23:34, when Jesus said, *"Father, forgive them, for they do not know what they are doing."*

Nothing I have been through compares to the emotional and physical pain of the abandonment, torture, pain, disappointment, loneliness, shame, and denial that Jesus felt when He hung on the cross. The people who saw Him display the power over all things left Him to suffer. What keeps my heart clear of unforgiveness is the cross. He suffered so that I would have eternal life. Surely the offenses the enemy wages against me through others don't compare.

The Lord also showed me to have mercy on those who offended me because they don't even know the devil is using them. Look at it this way: could it be that their own life is so far from God that their mind is the devil's playground?

As believers, we know there will be times of suffering and times of joy. During times of suffering, remember it is only temporary. A child of God cannot be a captive for long. If you find it hard to forgive, remember you need God's forgiveness daily from your tongue, emotions, and behavior.

Open Doors

Unforgiveness opens the door to the devil, which results in bringing judgment against you and hinders your relationship with God and His blessings. I operated that way for thirty-five years. Where did it come from? My own roots of childhood pain, rejection, bitterness, judgment, abandonment, shame, and anger led to unforgiveness. Thank God for His healing.

Areas to watch out for when you struggle with unforgiveness: vows, word curses, and judgment.

Vow

A vow is stating a word curse over somebody. You are trying to make a blood oath about them. This is a sin. Meaning of vow: a solemn promise, a pledge, a swear. As an example, a good vow is when you get married, have a child, become a judge, president, or hold a political office (well, maybe).

When you vow someone's demise, you are practicing witchcraft. You will be cursed and damned, so don't make vows. You are not God, nor are you Jesus or the Holy Spirit.

Example of a vow: "I vow or make the promise to kill or bring revenge for harm done to you." You may vow to never forgive: "I will never forgive you for your infidelity."

Release yourself from the vows.

Word Curse

A word curse can be spoken about oneself, others, places, or things. Others can speak a word curse about you.

Against One's Self:

- I'm not pretty enough.
- I'm dumb.
- I'll never get married.

Spoken Toward Others:

- My husband will never be faithful.
- That girl is jealous of me.
- That chick is ugly.
- All men cheat.
- You can't trust anybody.

Battle Zone

1. Think of a time you did not forgive
someone. How did it affect you emotionally,
physically, and spiritually?

_____

_____

_____

_____

_____

_____

2. Think of a time when you needed God's
forgiveness. Did you pray? Should you
forgive others before you pray to be forgiven?

_____

_____

_____

_____

_____

3. Can you forgive them now? Think of
three people you need to forgive for
their offenses.

_____

_____

_____

_____

4.   Pray to God for your forgiveness
for standing in judgment instead
of trusting God.

_____

_____

_____

_____

Scriptures on Forgiveness

Colossians 3:13
"Bear with each other and forgive one another if any of you has a grievance against someone.
Forgive as the Lord forgave you."

Ephesians 4:31-32
"Get rid of all bitterness, rage and anger, brawling and slander, along with every form of malice.
Be kind and compassionate to one another forgiving each other, just as in Christ God forgave
you."

If that didn't convince you, well, let's look at your obvious enemies. There is a word from God about them, too.

Matthew 5:44
"But I tell you, love your enemies and pray for those who persecute you."

Matthew 7:12
"So, in everything, do to others what you would have them do to you, for this sums up the Law
and the Prophets."

Proverbs 24:17
"Do not rejoice when your enemy fails, and do not let your heart be glad when he stumbles."

Mark 11:25-26
"Whenever you stand to pray, forgive; if you have anything against anyone so that your Father
who is in heaven will also forgive you your transgressions.

(But if you do not forgive, neither will your Father who is in heaven forgive your
transgressions.)"

That means I could be here living without God's covering of forgiveness because I didn't forgive somebody who offended me. Who is worth that? The person who offended me is not thinking about me at all. Secondly, they could have asked God for forgiveness and received it, and I'm still here in chains and bondage. Oh no, ladies, don't drag your past into your future and let everyone see your chains and bondage spoken out of your mouth.

In my training in Restoring the Foundation, there was a great definition of forgiveness:

- To grant relief from payment
- To pardon or excuse offense without penalty
- To cease feeling resentment against an offender.

Why is forgiveness necessary?

- God's word states it's expected of those who follow Christ.
- Forgiveness breaks the chains and brings freedom.
- You submit to God's judgment.

Battle Zone

1. Decide why forgiveness is the best
    way for your health, mind, and emotions.

_____

_____

_____

_____

_____

2. Pray daily to be forgiven of God
    for your own shortfalls.

_____

_____

_____

_____

_____

3. Meditate and speak the scriptures
    out loud in this prayer.

_____

_____

_____

_____

_____

☐ If you struggle with forgiving someone, share why your suffering was worse than what Jesus suffered on the cross.

Dear God Letters

If you have ex-husbands, boyfriends, baby daddies, siblings, coworkers, girlfriends, or parents, you may want to try a method I developed in Warrior Women TF called Dear God Letters.

Dear God letters are a great way to release emotions, pain, and feelings that you can't always share with an individual for many reasons. The Word states to cast your cares. Many people journal or keep diaries. You can do the same with Jesus. You will be shocked when you look back one to two years later and read where you were and how far the Lord has brought you.

People who suffer with being easily offended or those who have suffered at the hands of others in the past that led to trust issues will find comfort and a sense of release and healing writing to Jesus or God in the Dear God Letters. The women who've gone through Warrior Women TF training found a level of faith and intimacy in sharing and talking with Jesus. The weight of unforgiveness damages you physically, emotionally, and spiritually. It keeps you separated from God and His blessed son Jesus.

Share your Dear God Letters in the group and inspire others.

Chapter Four

Overcome Fear

This book is filled with many battles and God's role in each. You can't be a Warrior Woman unless you have fought in some battles. Your sword shouldn't be shiny and new. It should look worn and used. You may not have won all the battles, but you got up again. When you have been in a war, you gain experience on how to advance against your enemy. You learn about your weaknesses and strengths.

Fear is a powerful enemy upon all people, races, genders, and nations. Women have been fearful because of their lack of equal value and contributions to the world. Women are frozen in fear from speaking, sharing, and feeling secure in themselves. From the time they were children, women learn their value isn't as important as a boy in many cases. The first thing that enables you to stand and fight your battles is to gain strength in being fearless.

What Is Fear?

The word comes from the Greek word "*phobos*," meaning that which provokes a person to escape or run away. Another Greek word is "*deilia*" which means cowardice, shyness, and shame.

Fear is no respecter of family or person. We all have fears and/or are raised with fears. We are conditioned early to fear. Babies have no fear, children have few fears, but as parents, we instill in children what they should fear because of safety and many times, from our own experiences.

A Christian Warrior Woman is not a coward because a coward is a person who is afraid to act, take a stand, and/or represent what they know is the right thing to do. How many times do you hear a woman described as "brave" or "fearless"? Even a brave woman is afraid. But, she doesn't let her fears keep her frozen or hinder her from moving forward. I have found having a balance of fear can make you tenacious in moving forward.

The word in 2 Timothy 1:7 says, "For God has not given us a spirit of Fear." Romans 8:15 states, *"For you did not receive the spirit*

of bondage."

Fear is a stronghold that entraps you with fright, worry, anxiety, hesitation, procrastination, and unfruitfulness. Fear hinders your success in relationships, work, ministry, family, and future. Fear makes people cowards when they are faced with challenging circumstances that need action, decision, and taking a stand.

Jesus is our example of fearless because as He suffered, He didn't let His afflictions bring fear upon Him. He didn't even respond to their accusations. He knew why He was born, what He was supposed to do, and who was in control. What His accusers said didn't make His plans for His future and purpose change. Man did not inflict him with fear.

Women can learn greatly from this. When falsely accused, don't waste time arguing and justifying. Just do what God created you to do. The one thing I learned in my thirties was if I was going to fail, I'd fail doing what I believed was the right thing. I decided I would not fail following somebody else's plans or version of my truth.

What's Healthy Fear?

A natural fear of who is in control of your present, future, and family is healthy. This is where we fail, ladies. We fear Man who has only temporary control over you or your finances. You can choose what job you have, but you can't remove yourself from who created you.

There is only one person to fear, and that's God. When you fear man, it leads to:

- Not trusting God
- Lack of faith
- Control
- Being ashamed
- Jealousy
- Envy
- Murder
- Covetousness
- Stealing
- Robbing
- Lies

Too many ministers teach what man wants to hear by tingling ears and hearts with entertaining messages about giving to get earthly possessions. They want to be accepted because acceptance brings more members and more members bring more money. The Church should be where Jesus and the Holy Spirit dwell. Our lives should be transformed by the power of the congregation's faith. It has to be in us as individuals to bring it forth.

Earthly possessions should not be our motivation to serve and fear God. If we, the body, were living in holy fear when we come together, the power within each of us should manifest the Holy Spirit power in services. We should behold the healings, miracles, marriages saved, addictions healed, and cancer healed exploding in the service.

Churches are overrun with trying to meet the demands and needs of their congregations. God has not changed, healing has not changed, the word has not changed, so why is the church changing every year? If we are teaching the truth and have the power and authority, your congregation should need less of you and more of God. Is the Holy Spirit welcome? God never asked a hundred things. He asked for us to love Him and love each other. We need to examine why we welcome anything but the truth.

Ladies, this book is not about making the world or others love you more. It's about making your voice heard in a dark world full of crime, murder, violence, and abuse (sexual, mental and physical) toward women. It's time women rise up and speak to other women about their true worth and who God created them to be from their own personal experience. Each woman needs to feel that acceptance, confidence, and fearlessness about what she was created to do.

Her individual talents compliment every woman and man in the whole world. Every woman can't be a singer, dancer, preacher, inventor, lawyer, doctor, or writer, but she can be encouraged to explore her impact on the world. When Adam saw Eve, he was overwhelmed by her beauty. When the world sees you working, speaking, behaving in your identity, they will be in awe of your beauty as a woman, as well.

If you feel persecuted for being who you are, that is the price for your identity. That means God created you with the strength of a warrior to endure the challenges you will have. Jesus was persecuted for his identity and purpose. Why should you not feel overwhelmed at times? Remember everything you experience always has an end; make sure you win and persevere until the end with Christ.

You can only ensure your win by strategizing with God's plans and His word in prayer and standing still. God doesn't need your help. Trust me, I "helped" God for years, believing He was busy with the important people. I believed I needed to help myself. So many bad experiences lead you to believe you must do everything for yourself. That's the lie.

Fear is the first cousin to shame, who is related to worry, anxiety, nervousness, and is the second cousin to doubt.

My Fear

My excuse for taking two years to write this book was because I'd started to fear my future. I left corporate over ten years ago. My friends in corporate were retiring, buying fabulous homes, taking great vacations. A family member reminded me that I wasn't building up my retirement fund or preparing. I had been trusting God and seeing His wondrous works in other people and in me. The statement made me stop and think, *what am I doing for my future?*

I started to think about what I had planned for my future grandchildren, my kids, and about what I wanted to leave my children as a legacy from what I had accumulated. You see, the devil creeped into my thoughts unbeknownst to me. I started worrying, having regret and anxiety of what I might not be able to do or provide for myself in the future. It made me start applying for jobs to reclaim what I used to have. "Did I let regret creep in? Oh no!"

A woman who went through Warrior Women named Selena was very vocal and said, "Why would you think God wants you to go back to corporate? You are called to minister the gospel to the world." What Selena stated sounded right. I had let the spirit of fear creep in.

Also, the competitive side of me that made me successful couldn't bear that someone was making me feel lower or that I had less options than anybody else.

Do I have to remind you that I am not perfect and have to renew my mind daily against the schemes of the enemy, too?

For six months, I struggled with the worldly view of my identity versus my current ministry identity. I wasn't even happy in corporate. All the money, large house, cars, and social status came with a lot of pain. I was focused on the monetary benefit only of my past life. Thank God, He didn't let me wander far. I have so much more in my relationship, love, and fearless freedom than I ever had before.

After being exposed to God when I went back to work for a short time, I found people were as unimaginative, manipulative, unprofessional, and biased as they were ten years earlier. Returning made me realize I was far ahead of my peers in so many ways. It was unbelievable what God had done. I had gained more than any PhD would have provided. I gained more than man, a job, or a person could give me. I felt like I was on a mountaintop, and I had gone down to see the people living in a cave. Amen.

You and I are *Matthew 5:13-16* women:

"You are the salt of the earth, but if the salt has become tasteless, how can it be made salty again? It is no longer good for anything, except to be thrown out and trampled underfoot by men.

You are the light of the world. A city set on a hill cannot be hidden, nor does anyone light a lamp and put it under a basket, but on the lampstand, and it gives to all who are in the House. Let your light shine before men in such a way that they may see your good works and glorify your Father who is in heaven."

Women can no longer accept being marginalized, unheard, misunderstood, and treated shamefully. We carry forth an authority that pushes status and positions aside, allowing our light to shine brightly before all men. You are a beacon of hope for all the women in the world. Women of God do not let the world or church hush or quiet our calling.

Do not wait for a man or a woman to give you permission. If God has called you, the manifestation of His calling will be evident by all. I hope every young and mature woman reading this decides right now to be heard, not hidden. A light can't hide, so stop it.

Quote from Lisa

"When your fear in God grows due to faith and understanding Him and His word, your fear in man diminishes, which is the direction your soul longs for. God birthed you for His earthly and eternal plans."

Fear Is a Trap

There are so many things, people, and places to fear, but they are all a trap.

Psalms 27:1

"The Lord is my light and my salvation; whom shall I fear? The Lord is the strength of my life; of whom shall I be afraid?"

Proverbs 29:25

"Fearing People is a dangerous trap, but trusting the Lord means safety."

Hebrew 13:6

"The Lord is my helper; I will not be afraid. What can anyone do to me?"

Psalms 118:5-9

"The Lord is for me, so I will have no fear. What can mere people do to me? Yes, the Lord is for me; He will help me."

Women & Weak Words

The word "no" is not a curse, vow, or wrong. Women need to learn to say no without guilt or fear.

Women need to stop using the words, "I'm sorry" all the time. How often do you hear men say I'm sorry? Women take blame, shame, fear, and guilt into their daily language. Observe your language and word choices. Watch how often you say "sorry."

Galatians 1:10

"Am I saying this now to win the approval of people or God? Am I trying to please people? If I were still trying to please people, I would not be Christ's servant."

1 Thessalonians 2:4

"But as we were allowed of God to be put in trust with the gospel, even so we speak; not as pleasing men, but God, which trieth our hearts."

Other scriptures to review are *1 Deuteronomy 1:17, Exodus 23:2, Deuteronomy 31:6.*

Battle Zone

1. What are the three top fears operating
    in your life now?

_____

_____

_____

_____

_____

2. How will you overcome these fears?

_____

_____

_____

_____

_____

3. Why haven't you taken a stand on
    what you know is right?

_____

_____

_____

_____

4. What are you gaining with these fears?

_____

_____

_____

_____

_____

5. How does your fear for God manifest?

_____

_____

_____

_____

_____

6. What behaviors demonstrate you
    are a people pleaser?

_____

_____

_____

_____

_____

7. Name three things you must begin
    to combat Fear of Man.

_____

_____

_____

_____

_____

WARRIOR WOMEN - FEARLESS

2 Timothy 1:7

"For God gave us a spirit not of fear but of power and love and self-control."

Warrior Women Strength of the Past & Today

As you read below, ask yourself what you would do if serving God was against the law or prohibited? You can't be fearless unless you have faith. Has your faith grown, or are you in the same place you were in faith five years ago?

A relationship with God is full of continuous growth in areas of weakness and strength. When I ask people about their relationships with God, they tell me they are good with God. I know that is not the truth.

When you realize the magnitude of God in your life, you will feel so small in His abundance that "good" isn't the word to describe it.

Supernatural experiences are contagious and leave you desiring more of the heavenly exchange.

Fearless Women

Let's look at this article on fearless women. Be encouraged and gain strength from their faith. I can only pray to be this fearless when it's my time to represent the Lord Jesus Christ.

This is the article from: https://www.sharefaith.com/blog/2016/01/20-christian-woman-died-martyrs/

Felicitas (101 - 162)

Her life is celebrated on November 23 by both the Roman Catholic and Orthodox Churches. She and her seven sons were all martyred in Rome. Her tremendous conversion efforts were noticed by the pagan priests who then notified the emperor.

Before being martyred, she witnessed the death of each of her sons. The authorities gave her the opportunity to recant her witness after each son's death, but she refused.

Cecilia (~ 176)

Cecilia was a noblewoman in Rome who vowed herself to a life of celibacy. That was not her father's plan, and she was forced to marry instead. Her martyrdom came under Emperor Marcus Aurelius.

First, both her brothers were arrested and killed for refusing to sacrifice to the gods. After Cecilia was found to have converted more than four hundred people, she was condemned to die by heat (or suffocation) in the Roman baths. The fires were struck, and after a full day, she didn't even sweat.

An executioner came to behead her. He tried three times but could not complete it. After three days, she bled to death but never recanted her faith.

Blandina (162-177)

Blandina also died during the reign of Emperor Marcus Aurelius in the city of Lyon in Asia Minor. Blandina was arrested along with other Christians. She was a slave and not a Roman citizen. This is important because if she were a Roman citizen, her death would not include torture. A quick beheading should have been her fate.

Instead, she withstood so much torture that it is said the perpetrators became tired under her strength. Finally, she was taken to an Amphitheatre and bound to a stake. Wild animals were let loose. However, they did not touch her.

Days passed and finally, she was killed by throwing herself in front of a wild steer.

Perpetua (- 203)

Perpetua died in modern day Tunisia in Northern Africa (Carthage at the time). It was Emperor Septimius Severus's son's birthday, and Perpetua was one of several new Christian converts rounded up to celebrate the special day in a display of horrible violence. It's not known whether Severus was even involved. We do know that he put forward laws against conversion to Christianity.

Perpetua ultimately died by directing the gladiator's sword to her neck after being trampled and gored by a bull didn't work.

Catherine of Alexandria (287- 305)

At only eighteen years old, Catherine was converting hundreds to Christianity. And, when a persecution of Christians broke out, she tried to use her influence as the daughter of the Alexandrian governor to persuade the emperor. She went to the emperor and accused him of cruel acts.

He couldn't believe her boldness and called for fifty of the best pagan philosophers to debate her over her Christian beliefs. She won, and her fine-crafted arguments even converted some of the listeners. She was imprisoned. Two hundred visitors came to see her, including the emperor's wife. All were converted to Christianity.

She was condemned to die by the breaking wheel, but when she touched it, it fell to pieces. In frustration, she was finally beheaded.

Lucia of Syracuse (283-304)

The Diocletianic Persecution is also called the Great Persecution because it was the worst. Emperor Diocletian had the goal of wiping away Christianity forever. Lucia was one of thousands and thousands of people killed for their faith between 303 up until the toleration verdict by Constantine in 313.

Lucia refused to burn incense in worship of the governor of Syracuse, so she was sentenced to die. When the guards came to take her, they couldn't move her. They tried using an ox, but she would not budge. Then, they attempted to light her on fire where she sat, assembling straw around her. She wouldn't burn.

Finally, she died by sword.

Yes, there are centuries between these two entries. Many records of martyred women during this long period are difficult to locate with specificity. No doubt, whole swaths of Christians were killed for their faith during moments of conflict and persecution. As the Reformation unravels the Church, there is also martyrdom perpetrated from one Christian group to another.

Magdalene of Nagasaki (1611- October 16, 1634)

Magdalene would follow her parents as a martyr. Her parents died in 1620. During this period in Japan, Christianity was outlawed, and the penalty was death. Since she was only nine when she lost her parents, she received much counsel from two Augustinian friars who were also martyred.

At the age of twenty-three, she decided to surrender to authorities and publicly declare herself a follower of Jesus. After thirteen days of torture, she was strangled to death in a hole upside down.

Narcissa Prentiss Whitman

(March 14, 1808 – Nov 29, 1847)

Narcissa served as a missionary to the Oregon territory. She was the first white woman to make the journey. She wanted to bring the message of Jesus to the native Cayuse and Nez Perce tribes in what is now Walla Walla, Washington.

There was already a fort near their mission site, and she and her husband Marcus, a doctor, were to care for and evangelize the tribal people. They spent eleven years in ministry.

They ended up dying by the hand of Tiloukaikt and his men. Their suspicion of the white people not dying of measles like his people was more than unfortunate since immunity due to past exposure had everything to do with the reason.

Lucy Yi Zhenmei (Dec. 9, 1815 – Feb. 19, 1862)

Lucy was born to a Catholic family in China. She committed her life to Christ at a young age and worked to support her family, as well as teaching the women at her parish. She was enthusiastic about evangelism despite the dangers she knew about should the authorities discover her fervor.

In 1861, she worked with Father Wen Nair to establish a mission in Jiashan Long. In that area, the provincial governor began to arrest Christians and ask them to renounce their faith. Father Nair and others in the mission, including Lucy, were arrested and sentenced to death without a trial.

They all were beheaded the next day.

Edith Stein (October 12, 1891 – August 9, 1942)

As a German Jew who'd converted to Christianity during the tumultuous time of World War II, Edith soon knew the dangers of her ethnicity and her newfound faith. She became a nun and taught school in Speyer.

By 1933, the Nazis passed laws that prohibited any non-Aryan person from civil service. Edith and her sister were moved to a Netherlands monastery for their safety, but in 1942, the Nazis arrested them and sentenced both women to Auschwitz.

They died seven days later in the gas chambers.

Esther John (Dec. 14, 1929 – Feb. 2, 1960)

Esther served as a nurse in Pakistan. She was born into an Islamic family in British India but converted at age seventeen after she'd read Isaiah in Christian school. Her family moved to the new country of Pakistan in 1947.

Fearing an arranged Muslim wedding, she left home and changed her name. She began work with orphans and then at a mission hospital, evangelizing in the nearby villages. She was found murdered at her home.

Though no one was arrested for the crime, the suspicion is that Esther's brothers found her and killed her because of her Christianity and disobedience to Islam.

Two in Pakistan (September 22, 2013)

In Peshawar, Pakistan, stands All Saints Church, a church sharing the love of Jesus since 1883. On September 22, 2013, two Islamic suicide bombers entered the church. Eighty-one Christians were killed in one of the deadliest attacks ever on the Christian community in Pakistan.

The two sisters pictured were among the victims. They were new to the family of God, only recently accepting faith in Jesus after receiving a copy of "The Story of Jesus," a booklet that explained the Gospel.

Mary Sameh George (- March 28, 2014)

Mary traveled to Cairo, Egypt, to help a poor family with their basic needs. On March 28, 2014, this Christian service brought the ultimate sacrifice. "Once they saw that she was a Christian [because of the cross hanging on her rear-view mirror], they jumped on top of the car, to the point that the vehicle was no longer visible," an eyewitness said, as reported by The Voice of the Martyrs.

"The roof of the car collapsed. When they realized that she was starting to die, they pulled her out of the car and started pounding on her and pulling her hair, to the point that portions of her hair and scalp came off. They kept beating her, kicking her, stabbing her with any object or weapon they could find."

It is also known that Mary was shot, and her car burned.

Suffiia (Unknown –- April 2014)

Sufia, a young Christian woman in Somalia, was killed in Mogadishu. She was dragged from her home by armed men who shot her and then fled. Her only offence was her Christian faith.

According to The Voice of Martyrs, Somalia is second only to North Korea as the worst persecutors of Christians. In fact, a Muslim group in Somalia with allegiance to Al Qaeda has sworn to rid their country of all Christians. So, certain death will come even if a piece of Christian literature is found associated with a person.

Sufia is not the real name of this Christian woman who died for her faith, in case the perpetrators uncover others associated with her.

SEIJA JARVENPAA and KAIJA LIISA MARTIN (-JULY 24, 2014)

Seija and Kaija, both from Finland, worked for International Assistance Mission (IAM), an international Christian organization that has served the people of Afghanistan through health and economic development since 1966. They both had more than fifteen years of service with the ministry, Seija with mental health patients and Kaija with low income women in business development.

In July of 2014, because of their work and identity, they were both killed in Herat by ISIS.

Shama and her husband, Shehzad Masih

(- November 4, 2014)

The village of Kot Radha Kishan in the Punjab province of Pakistan saw great violence the night a mob came for Shama and Shehzad. There was a rumor that this Christian couple burned a copy of the Quran. It was a grievance that the owner of a local kiln knew he could make when a dispute arose about them owing him money.

The angry mob came for them even though their Christian witness was without repute. Shama also was pregnant with their fourth child. They were burned alive in the kiln at such a high temperature nothing remained. Their three children are now with relatives, and the ten other Christian families in the village have fled, seeking some retribution against similar accusations.

Neima Abiad Idris (1965-November 6, 2014)

Known as the Peace Singer in her Sudan village of Kadir, in the Nuba Mountains, Neima wrote songs, leading a choir of ladies in her native Koliib that expressed peace and forgiveness, faith and perseverance.

She didn't run away even though genocidal terror was targeting her and her family in the war zone that she called home. Even though it would be easier to flee to a garrison city, she sought reconciliation with the Islamic warring factions by demonstrating a Christian witness of her word and witness.

She died from a bomb that hit her home.

Kayla Mueller (August 14, 1988 – February 6, 2015)

Kayla went to Jordan as a humanitarian worker. From Prescott, Arizona, Kayla didn't expect that her faith would be tried and ultimately strengthened through an ordeal of capture, sexual torture, and ultimate death.

Held by ISIS leader Abu Bakr al-Baghdadi, she sheltered two other girls from additional harm, and when a chance for escape came, she decided to stay, telling the other two that her American appearance would endanger them.

Soon afterward, she was killed. She wrote in a letter, "I have surrendered myself to our creator b/c literally there was no else....+ by God + by your prayers I have felt tenderly cradled in free fall."

Depayne Middleton-Doctor (49), Ethel Lee Lance (70), Myra Thompson (59), Sharonda Coleman-Singleton (45), Susie Jackson (87), Cynthia Marie Graham Hurd (54), (--June 17, 2015)

The Bible study group was happy to invite in Dylann Roof into their group that night at Emanuel AME Church. The church has been a beacon for the love of Jesus since 1816, and even through the tragedy of their guest returning to kill nine parishioners, including these six women and the senior pastor, it's with complete confidence that we can say God will continue to use the church for His greater glory.

The reaction of the church community is testimony to this, for as others might viciously hate the killer and everything he represents, they've asked for forgiveness and renewal in the life of the community at large.

(Wikipedia was helpful with the information from centuries gone by. The Voice of the Martyrs, http://www.persecution.com, a site we'd encourage you to visit, was helpful in uncovering today's recently martyred)

***

BE BOLD

I was working in holistic health, and coincidently, I was pursuing God and fasting when I began. The Lord showed me the blueprint and how to start my business. God knew He was leading me into the healing arena but took me through the steps that grew my faith from the physical to supernatural.

I had a new client who had been in a couple of times for a colonic. During a session, she told me she felt strange and uneasy. I was naïve to the power of fasting and prayer on others, so I didn't know I was affecting her.

After the session, she went to the restroom. I waited to check her out in the office and get payment. She took a very long time to come out. I went near the restroom to see if she was all right. I heard her talking to herself in multiple voices. I was stunned. I had hoped she was on the phone, but she wasn't.

I called out to her to ask if she was all right, and a nervous voice responded back. I was like, "Jesus, this can't be happening in my bathroom!" I waited in the office wondering what the woman was going through. She finally entered my office but kept her head down, refusing to make eye contact.

I asked her if she was okay. She grunted and nodded, never looking up at me. She handed me her credit card and still wouldn't look up. She told me she had never had an experience like the one I'd given her. I could tell she was in a hurry to escape, but from what, I didn't understand.

I got up to walk her out the door because she was trying to get out before I could come near her. As we both were going through the French doors, I don't know if I touched her, but our closeness made her startled for a second, and she glanced nervously at where I was going. As she glanced up quickly in fear at me, I saw the eyes of a demon.

Her eyes were like an orange color with black slashes.

They weren't her eyes. Something was in her. She stunned me, so I stood there like, "What did I just see? Are you kidding me?" She hurried past me and left. I stood in shock of what I had just seen with my own eyes, but I wasn't afraid.

During fasting, I learned the Holy Spirit operates fearlessly in my body while my flesh yells, "Run away, Lisa." I stood there watching her walk. I searched my mind because I knew what I'd seen. While I was standing there, the Holy Spirit said, "Go after her." Here is where I need a comedian to do a face that looks like, "Whaaaaat?!?"

I instantly responded with, "I'm not trained in that kind of ministry work. I am not a minister." My excuses flooded the mainframe of my mind.

The Lord said, "You are qualified."

I worried I wasn't able. You are supposed to have two people when dealing with people like that.

The Lord spokes. "Look at her. You are qualified."

I looked out the door that was still open. She hadn't driven away. She was holding the wheel tightly, looking angry. I tried pleading again with Jesus. I wouldn't know what to say.

The Lord said, "Don't worry. It will come to you."

I looked, and she was still there. Lord, why hadn't she driven away? My flesh was screaming, "Run away, Lisa. You aren't qualified. We ain't going over there!" The Holy Spirit in me had a Madea twang, like, "Did some demon show up at my house when he knows I'm a friend of Jesus?"

I walked to the car without a clue as to what I was going to say. She saw me outside her window and rolled it down. She started crying. She had tried everything to get rid of this thing within her. She stated, "I have traveled to many countries and got no relief." She said, "I had hoped you could help me, but it's still here."

The Holy Spirit decided to answer using my vessel because, just being honest, my flesh was not comfortable. My mouth spoke and asked her, "Have you tried Jesus?" I was very confident and emboldened in the spirit while my flesh had my eyes covered, telling me to let it know when the scary part was over.

This is when the battle began. Her response felt like somebody had cursed my momma. She turned her head like a snake with her eyes blazingly wide and yelled out, "Jesus! Jesus! Jesus won't help me! Jesus gave me a husband that set me on fire on Christmas day!" Her face, her demeanor, her rage about Jesus welled up at me like a personal attack.

A boldness from God that wanted to beat whatever demon was in her for lying about Jesus rose within me. I was ready for a fight. I felt a raging flame being ignited in my chest. How dare she speak His name in that manner?

I calmly and lovingly asked her one question ... "Did Jesus give you your husband, or did you marry the guy you desired with no regard to Jesus during your decision? Did you not willingly marry him?"

At this point and prior, that thing in her was looking and talking with me. After I asked the simple question, I literally saw her whole body and demeanor change instantly. The demon left her immediately when faced with the truth. She dropped her head and cried on her wheel, saying, "I was wrong. I didn't ask Jesus."

I knew I was now talking with the woman and not the demon in her. I asked her if I could pray for her. She said yes, and I prayed. I had her pray the sinner's prayer. She felt embarrassed. I told her everything was okay. I assured her Jesus loved her.

She shared she knew the Bible. She'd lost faith due to an abusive husband that made her life hell on earth. As I walked back in my office, I smiled because God used me to set a captive free. I rejoiced and was thankful. When it was over, I said, "What in the world did I just experience?"

I don't even like horror movies or vampire stories. The Lord was proud of me that day. He said, "You let Me use you to bring healing." I learned from the Lord it's not about how I feel or what I know. It's about what He wants to do in somebody's life that matters. I prayed to be used by Him again in the miraculous, and He continues to excite me.

Chapter Five

Faith

Scripture Hebrews 11:6

"And without Faith, it is impossible to please God, because anyone that comes to Him must believe that He exists and that He rewards those who earnestly seek him."

I shared my personal experiences because the enemy comes early in our lives while we are young, trusting, and believing. His goal is to create painful scenarios early to make us lose faith. We come into the world trusting, hopeful, happy, and believing.

The definition of "faith," according to Webster, mentions loyal, true, and constant. Hebrews 11:11 lays out the meaning as God describes it. Please open your Bible, and while you read, ask yourself, "Where is my faith?" Don't beat yourself up, though. That's why this book is in your hands.

Jesus is going to raise your level of faith. If the holiest person you know was reading this chapter, he or she would find opportunities to improve. We all fall short of the glory of God. That's why we always need to mature and grow in faith. You can't fight any battle or take back your life without faith. You can't please God without faith.

Children have faith their mothers will feed them. They know her smell and cry when she leaves because the mother has continually been feeding the child which led to trust. As that child gets older, the enemy's plan is to make the child lose faith in what they know.

It can be a challenge to have faith in God when your parents have not been protective or trusting in your early years. It's hard to trust God when Daddy abandoned or abused you. The truth is, you can forgive and find healing no matter what your circumstances are. People like to say it often, but living it is very different.

My faith came alive when my relationship with God was based on day-to-day experiences with Him activated in my life.

Women of FAITH

Eloise was a married Christian working mom with two small boys. She believed in her husband and the future of their family. One day, Eloise's husband, George, came home from work and told her he was leaving her and the two kids for another woman.

He claimed he was in love with his supervisor. Eloise was shocked, upset, and couldn't believe he would leave her with two small children for another woman. She was devastated to learn his co-workers and others knew of the affair. She felt betrayed, embarrassed, stupid, confused, and angry that this could happen to her.

George stated he would be filing and obtaining a divorce ASAP. He showed no compassion but stated it as a matter of fact. Eloise, although feeling rejected, disappointed, and alone stood still. She continued to work, take care of her kids, and planned on letting him do what he'd stated.

Three months later, George received shocking and alarming news from his doctor during a routine checkup. He learned he had an advanced level of prostate cancer and would need surgery soon. George continued his affair.

The doctor recommended immediate surgery for his prostate cancer diagnosis. The other woman was in the hospital with George when he awakened from surgery. George called his wife while the other woman was at his side. Eloise asked if she could come to the hospital. George told her she could. When Eloise arrived, the other woman was not present.

As George was being discharged from the hospital, he decided to go home with his wife. The Lord had shown George he was wrong for breaking covenant with his wife and sons. He knew what was happening to him was God's judgment, and he needed to rethink his steps and actions.

After George was home, the other woman called to check on him. Eloise heard George tell the other woman not to call him again. He told her the affair was over and he'd made the choice to stay with his family and his wife. He would be restoring the damage he had done.

Eloise was surprised and didn't know if she should trust him. She knew marriage was supposed to be for better or worse. She had seen the worst and wondered if better was possible after the devastating news of an affair. Could she trust him again?

She felt the wound of his betrayal and mixed emotions for a while. God strengthened her to feel secure in their marriage. George never recovered fully and would be sick for the next twenty years until his death. Eloise sacrificed and took care of him as a loving wife.

I can imagine what you are thinking. What would you have done? I commend Eloise for the strength to endure and keep her family intact. George dealt a devastating blow that affected Eloise and her children for twenty years.

Sin affects not only you but your loved ones. George's children had to live with their father's sickness, as well. If George didn't cheat, would he not have gotten prostate cancer? We will never know. We do know that Eloise is a woman of faith. She could have easily stated, "I have Biblical and legal grounds for a divorce." But she chose to forgive and trust George. George never gave her reason again to distrust him in their marriage.

Maybe you have or had a husband who struggles/ed with infidelity. Faith is a gift from God. Eloise is alive today to share what she endured. At the age of eighty-five, she is alive to see her grandchildren. She lived to receive other miracles in her life.

You, too, can forgive those who have hurt or wounded you. It takes time but make it your mission to heal. Wounded people wound other people. Stop the madness now.

Battle Zone

1. What are your thoughts about Eloise?

_____

_____

_____

_____

2. Can you relate to Eloise?

_____

_____

_____

_____

3. What would you have done if you
were Eloise?

_____

_____

_____

_____

4. Who was Eloise faithful to?

_____

_____

_____

_____

5. Describe what you found unforgivable.

_____

_____

_____

_____

_____

6.   Would Eloise have been wrong if
        she left George?

_____

_____

_____

_____

7.   How have you dealt with infidelity,
        pornography, or online cheating?

_____

_____

_____

_____

8.   What will you ask God to do about
        your George type?

_____

_____

_____

_____

9.   What do you have faith in?

_____

_____

_____

LIVE BY FAITH

Hebrews 11:1

"Now faith is confidence in what we hope for and assurance about what we do not see. This is what the ancients were commended for."

Faith isn't what we already have or know. That's not faith; that's evidence. Faith is in God's promises through His word. I will outline what's promised in this chapter. God's promises are throughout the whole Bible.

Verse 1 & 2:

Confidence – In whom do you have confidence?

Verse 3:

God as the creator of all things. He is in control.

Verse 4:

Testimony transcends time, generational blessings.

Verse 5-6:

To please God is to love God.

Verse 7:

Obey God.

Verse 8:

We are all called to listen, go, and obey God.

Verse 11:

The power of faith makes impossible, possible.
A barren woman becomes boundless.

Verse 12:

God's word fulfilled by Abraham. Muslims,
Christians, and other religions claim Abraham
as their father of faith. The promise that
Abraham did not witness, but God's word is
always fulfilled. Generational blessing.

Verse 17:

Blind faith. You may not understand all that
God is saying to you at the exact moment.
Faith = Trust.

Verse 19:

> Faith can resurrect you out of your darkest
> hour of pain to your greatest dreams and desires.
> Abraham believed it could happen.

Verse 20:

> Parents can speak generational blessings and
> have faith in their fulfillment.

Verse 21:

> Your faith can see you through until your
> last words are spoken.

Verse 22:

> Faith allows you to accept your fate and the
> dreams of your family's future.

Verse 23:

> Faith makes you fearless in all circumstances
> with family, friends, and the law.

Verse 24:

> Faith brings identity.

Verse 25:

> Faith provides strength in times of struggle.

Verse 26:

> Faith provides vision for eternal purpose
> versus current condition.

Verse 27:

> Faith creates fearless attitude toward your
> past and future.

Verse 28-29:

> Faith can save your family, race, and
> country from your enemy.

Verse 30:

> Faith opens the door to hearing from God
> and brings reward and victory.

Verse 31:

> Faith removes the shame of sin and brings a
> new beginning.

Verse 32-33:

> Faith makes you a Warrior Woman. Faith
> conquers kingdoms (fears), brings justice, security,
> safety into your job, personal life, marriage,
> children, and church.

Verse 34-35:

> Faith gives you the strength and the shield to
> stand for Christ, even when you are under
> pressure. Faith can lead to dying for your beliefs.

How do you get this faith? Faith comes from trust and life experience. It comes from failing and falling short. It comes from seeing the truth about how God is in every circumstance, speaking and providing signs, if we only remove the scales, remove the wax, and trust our inner female voice.

Faith comes from the daily interaction of prayer, reading the bible, extending faith, trusting God, and meditation.

Testimony

Think of areas where you lack faith, your family lacks faith, and your children lack faith. If this continues, will you overcome it or keep losing the battle?

Faith "Suddenly"

This testimony is for anyone suffering sickness, disability, or an attack of some type in your life.

I was attending a three-month internship with the International House of Prayer, Atlanta, in 2010. I was the oldest intern, considering the majority; everybody else was eighteen to twenty-five years old. I had observed a young lady on staff that I had sensed may have been leading a young man on by allowing him to do things for her that weren't appropriate if you aren't in a relationship. I pulled her aside privately and gave her advice. It was received, and she confirmed her intentions were not the same as his.

Later at the evening service, I was assisting the director and praying over the people who had come down to the altar for prayer. People were falling out, and God was bringing healing to a lot of young people. As the director approached the young lady I had advised earlier, suddenly, her body came at me like a freight train.

I'm not some petite little thing, but I didn't see her coming at me. The force of her body threw me backward, and I hit the raised edge of the stage. I hit so hard that the middle of my back bounced me off the stage and onto the floor.

The problem in some churches is that people can think the Holy Spirit knocked you out when it didn't. The spirit in the young lady jumped me, and now I was lying on the floor at the altar and couldn't move. My back was in serious pain as I laid there.

I saw people praising God and looking at me as if God knocked me down. Did He? I couldn't talk above a whisper without pain. I laid there thinking, "What should I do?" I knew this was serious.

I closed my eyes, trying to relax, even in the pain. People came over touching me, laughing that I was flat on my back in the Spirit. They had no clue I was really hurt. After I realized nobody had figured it out, I said, "Lord, help me." The music, the talking, and the noise got softer.

I heard the Spirit say, "You cannot go to the hospital. Trust me."

I was thinking, I can't move. How will I not go to the hospital? People will realize I can't move. This doesn't make sense.

I heard the Spirit say, "Do not go to the hospital. Trust God."

After about an hour and a half, the training director realized I was on the ground by the altar but not moving. He came over to me and said, "Lisa, are you okay?" He bent down and said again, "Are you okay?"

I told him that I couldn't move. He beckoned to his brother, who was built like a linebacker, to help. They tried to move me, and a wretched pain struck me. I yelled, "NO!" They said I needed an ambulance. But I remembered the Spirit had said there was to be no ambulance. So, I told them, "No ambulance."

My son, Amiri, came over and said, "Mom, you can't get home this way."

I told him we would manage. I asked someone to bring my car to the front. They got me up and dragged my body to the car. I had a BMW X5, so I didn't have to bend once they laid the seat back, put my legs in, and asked if I was okay. I realize, looking back, that they asked again if I was okay while others stated that I needed an ambulance. It's a miracle I got in the car. I drove home in such horrible pain.

My son asked, "How will you get in the townhouse and up the stairs?"

I told him I would figure out a way. When I got home, I slid out of the car with my son's help. I walked alongside the wall of the stairs, trying to get to the bedroom with my son's help for nearly an hour.

It was God that helped me deal with the striking sharp pain. I realized I had to use the bathroom. When I got to the third floor of the townhouse, bending to reach the toilet was not an option. I asked my son to turn on the shower. Thank God it was a walk-in.

I couldn't bend to take off my clothes. My son took off my shoes, and I asked him to leave my bathroom. He was worried and said, "You need to go to the hospital."

I didn't want him to be alarmed. I prayed and cried, "Lord, help me." I walked into the shower with my clothes on because I had to pee, and there was no stopping me now. I was laid out for two hours on the church altar, forty-five minutes getting up and to the car, forty minutes driving home, and one hour getting up to my bedroom.

I stood in the shower with my clothes on, peeling them off as the hot water ran down my body. I walked slowly and thanked God I had a high bed. I screamed and fell backward. I lay wondering what I was doing. I could be seriously injured, and people would think I had lost my mind.

I was sure I'd heard, "Don't call an ambulance; don't go to the hospital." What if the devil was tricking me? What if I was wrong? The longer I waited, the more damage could happen. I went to sleep and woke up around 7 a.m.

What do we all have to do when we wake up in the morning? Yes, I woke up wanting to go to the bathroom. I couldn't move more than an inch at a time. The pain was even worse. Forty-five minutes later, I was still not even at the edge of the bed.

I realized my best bet was to roll off the bed, fall to the carpet, and try to crawl to the bathroom. As I fell to the floor, I knew I couldn't crawl. I couldn't make it to the bathroom. I called to my son to bring me a pot, but I couldn't move to lift myself up to use the pot.

I told my son to pass me my cell phone, and then leave. I felt defeated because I couldn't hold my bowels any longer. I had to let go, and I laid there in my mess. I cried because I was in such pain.

As I laid there, a voice started to taunt me, saying, "You used to be a big-time executive making crazy money. Now you lay there in your mess—alone—because you thought you could go into ministry. You can't even walk now. Imagine if your corporate friends could see you now."

I started to pray, quoted scripture, and said, "Get thee behind me, Satan."

I called my ex-husband, who lived in Chattanooga, Tennessee, two hours away, and I told him what had happened and that I was on the floor. He told me to call the ambulance, but I explained that I couldn't go to the hospital. I asked him to please help me.

Two and half hours later, Andre was looking at me, lying in the same spot. He said, "Lisa, you can't move. This is ridiculous!"

He dragged me to my feet, and I begged him to stop because of the pain. I was back in the shower again. My ex-husband cleaned up the carpet and helped wash me. He dried me off and dressed me. He stayed until the next morning when he had to go to work.

Tuesday came, and some of my other interns called to bring food or come over. But I couldn't get to the door or walk downstairs. I didn't call my mom or any of my family members because they would have thought I was crazy. As I laid there heading into Day Four of the back pain, I felt that because the devil had mocked me, I had renewed determination.

I knew that I had heard God, and if this was my new future, everything would be different. I evaluated everything I had heard, seen, and experienced, and I believed one thing. I had faith in God. I was a ministry intern, and I felt at the height of my faith level.

The devil came to destroy me and take my faith in God away. This happened on a Sunday, and it was now Thursday. I asked my son if he would open the windows in my room I knew nobody would understand what I had done.

As I told myself that even if I were to fail because I'd put my hope and trust in God, I was still in a good place. That afternoon as I looked out the window, the sun looked beautiful. This was a journey that only I could understand, and I was the only one who could see it through. I felt determined despite hearing everyone else's doubt. I explained to my ex-husband what God had told me.

He confirmed, "You do hear him, so we shall see."

As I looked out the window into the sun, I said, "I trust you."

I felt a fullness of love, trust, and belief that no matter what came, God was real for me. The Word was deep in my heart. I had been on this journey for deeper knowledge and power for two years, and I had seen miracles in others.

As I looked at the sky through my windows and marveled at the beauty of the sun, created by God the rays flooded into my room. It had a simple smile on my face, knowing God is real when *suddenly* I felt a presence. I felt a presence on the right side of my bed. I could sense something was standing at the middle section of the bed with its back to the window where I was gazing at the sun. All sudden I heard a sound over my body that sounded like an electric wand, buzzing over me like a scanner from head to toe.

The wand started at my head and moved over my total body toward my feet. When it stopped, I sat up and my back was healed.

There was no pain. How could this be? I sat there for a second and said, "Lord Jesus, you healed me?!"

I called out to my son.

"Are you in pain?" he said, shocked to see me sitting up.

"No," I said. "Jesus healed me. I have no pain. I was unable to walk, and now I can walk."

I had no pain anywhere. I moved my back every which way, and it was totally healed instantly. I'll never forget the sound of the wand over my body. I testified of my healing at International House of Prayer the next weekend.

If you have breast cancer, high blood pressure, diabetes, or paralysis, God can heal you instantly. I can bear witness that instant healing is available to you, your family, or a friend. Trust God. He is faithful. After you go through this book, you will be at a new level of faith, and regardless of what you need, He will provide for you. Will you trust Him for your children, your marriage, your job, and your finances? Raise your level of faith through reading, hearing, and singing about your relationship with God.

Next, let's talk about your relationship with God because that is what raised my faith to an unimaginable level. I ask myself now if my faith is as high as it was then. I passed that challenge of faith and felt so incredibly supernatural that I was speechless. Ladies, is it time for your supernatural healing through faith?

You must command your day, thoughts, and activities to achieve your goal. God will give you the ability to self-coach and self-motivate yourself to press on when it's tough. Christian Warrior Women training is for women who are tired of being a watcher of other's success. A Warrior Woman decides to be a focused and active participant in her own life.

Battle Zone

1. On a scale from one to ten with ten being the highest, what is your faith level? Why?

_____
_____
_____
_____
_____

2. Explain areas in your life where you need faith and Trust in God.

_____
_____
_____
_____
_____

3. Why have you lost faith?

_____
_____
_____
_____
_____

Pray

Jesus, create in me a new heart, new ears, new eyes to see, believe, hear, and trust you in all areas of my life. My hope needs to be set on nothing else but Jesus Christ and his righteousness.

Lord, I use my tongue to speak life upon these dry bones. I declare my victory is not in the words of man but in every word written in the bible and upon my heart as a believer. I declare healing of:

1.) _____

2.) _____

Repeat until you feel your spirit rise with power and confidence.

Hebrews 11:1

"Now faith is confidence in what we hope for and assurance about what we do not see."

Personal Faith Exercise

I am going to give you something to think about when it comes to faith. I'm going to show you a quick and easy way to judge your faith. Your faith is based on what you say, want, and act on.

If you examine your day...

- What time do you wake up?
- How do you normally feel when you wake up?
- Who do you talk to first?
- How much time is there from when you wake up 'til you leave for work in the morning?
- Where do you work?
- How do you feel about your work? The people at your job?
- What do you say to yourself about your job in a typical day?
- How do you talk to others in a typical day?
- Examine your emotions in a typical day.
- Are you upset about something daily?
- What time do you leave work?
- What do you do the first three hours after work?
- How many hours of TV do you watch?
- How much time do you spend on the phone talking outside of work?
- How many hours a day do you text or have your cell phone in your hand?
- How many hours do you spend on social media?

After you answer the above, add up the total hours from the last four questions. The one thing about faith is it requires your time. Your belief yields words and influence. What you believe is spoken every day, whether good or bad?

Number of hours: _____.

We always make faith about religious aspects of our lives. Every person alive has faith in many things. If we dig deeper in evaluating where your time is spent, idolatry may have a stronghold in your life.

POWER OF WORDS

Affirmation

Affirmation can mean declaring, announcing, and proclaiming. It can also be an emotional affirmation such as a father affirming his daughter is beautiful. I received affirmation from my father that I was double trouble: smarter than a man and beautiful.

If I had a father that said I was ugly and dumb, that would not be an affirmation. People associate affirmation with the positive. Women affirm themselves every day, but is it positive? Every day that you complain, get angry, feel like a victim, or feel life is cheating you, it's being affirmed into your life. You are also drawing in more of what you speak into your life.

Who or what you believe in your heart is what you are receiving when you do it in your strength. Many Christians are trapped in their gut beliefs about themselves which do not line up with the Word. Your success begins with realigning and renewing your affirming mindset, behaviors, and self-talk.

Example: What do you tell people about yourself every day? I am fat! I am lonely! I'll never meet a man! My marriage sucks! I am not smart! I'm not pretty!

What does God say about you to affirm you? Should you not speak what is true? Do you speak affirming words from others that bring death to your dreams? Faith is a hard word.

As believers, we spend time thinking about what the devil is doing, but most of the overcoming is about our actions. We can't blame the devil for not setting the alarm clock, not turning off the TV, laziness, or procrastination. Your faith is lacking because you choose to watch and let life happen.

A Christian Warrior Woman prays and grows in faith by doing what she deems her Father in Heaven has said. Can you miss or not understand? Yes. What I have found is patience is a skill. To wait on the Lord to answer can be difficult. When you let your own emotions, desires, and flesh take charge, we lose.

I used to think God needed my help. I thought faith was helping God, so He could spend time with important people. God does not need our help. We need His. Affirm yourself with His word. And for the people who speak words about you that don't line up with the Word? You need to stop them before they speak it in love or ignore and pray the words off immediately.

Word Curses

A word curse is not just vulgar language spoken toward you like getting cursed out. Word curses are also words spoken over you that limit your potential such as "Girl, you can't model. You're not pretty enough," or "You can't sing," or "You can't be President," or "You can't own a business." I learned early, thanks to God, to tune out word curses from relatives and friends.

Example: Break agreement with the word curse spoken over you that you will never get married. Or, break the word curse that you will always be in poverty with a bunch of kids. Or, you won't get a loan for a mortgage.

Stop the madness and declare the opposite. *I can do all things through Christ that strengthens me!*

When we are low, people tell us that we don't have enough faith. It sounds like religious speak. Most of the time, the people telling us don't know how to advise us, so when in doubt, they tell others to have faith. I am going to share with you how the Lord showed me to have faith and introduce you to Hebrews 11:11, one of many bible scripture passages that made it clear to me.

First, while in prayer seeking God, my experience and the Word became one.

"And without Faith, it is impossible to please God, because anyone that comes to Him must believe that He exists and that He rewards those who earnestly seek him." (Hebrews 11:6)

This is the key piece of armor to bear before your opponent, the devil.

Chapter Six

Relationship with God

Psalms 14:2
"The Lord looks down from heaven on all mankind to see if there are any who understand, any who seek God."

Deuteronomy 4:29-30
"But if from there you seek the Lord your God, you will find him if you seek him with all your heart and with all your soul. When you are in distress and all these things have happened to you, then in later days you will return to the Lord your God and obey him."

This is a difficult chapter because there is so much I want to share and tell you about how amazingly confident and special you'll feel when you know that Jesus talks and shares secrets with you. I did not know He had been sharing words with me my whole life. I know He has been talking to you, as well.

In this section, I am going to talk about where I began in pursuing my relationship with Jesus and the manifestations that followed. I am going to share what I did and then what Jesus did to respond to my seeking.

The first step is deciding to accept Christ as your Lord and Savior.

The Choice

Each of you must choose to believe, serve, and worship God. I am not asking you to follow man, a church, or religion. If you want to see your life become limitless, fearless, and courageous you need to hang with like-minded people.

My father told me, "If you want to be smart, hang with smart people. If you want to be rich, hang with rich people." If you want the power of God that He promises each of us, you need to spend time with God the Father, Son and Holy Spirit. You find God by reading all the promises He has made to you. You will find your life in His word.

Battle Zone Prayer

Say these words out loud:

"Lord Jesus, I choose to seek You, find You, believe You, and put my trust in You in good and bad days. Lord, I repent for living by my rules instead of honoring myself as a woman with exceptional gifts and talents that You have blessed me with."

By 2005, with the loss of my grandmother, my stroke, migraines, and the memories of Jesus saving me, I wanted to know why. Why had I gone through this? These are just a sample of things that happened to me.

I wanted to know that God, Jesus, and the Holy Spirit were real on a personal level. I didn't want tradition, religion, or words spoken by others to control my thinking or behavior. I was hungry for something greater than I'd experienced. I didn't want just Sunday service and giving generously. I had a burning desire to seek Him out until I found Him.

I wanted to feel what my grandmother had felt. I had a voice in my head that had been speaking to me since I was a child. I didn't know anybody else testifying or mentioning this. Why was He protecting and talking to me?

The questions were endless about my grandmother's relationship with God:

- What made her cry?
- What made her stay on her knees and call out family and friend's names three times a day?
- What made her sing to Jesus every day?
- Was He hearing her prayers?
- Why was she confident?
- Why had she memorized the entire Bible?

I had to know the answers to my questions in a purposeful manner. I was determined to see my grandmother again. I had the role model of a woman who knew Jesus in my life.

The journey began with God showing me the church I would join in Atlanta, Georgia. I lived in Johns Creek, and the Lord literally spoke to me when I landed on the website page of Victory World Church in Norcross.

I knew after the first service that I'd found the church for me. I would become a member and serve in many capacities of leadership in areas such as youth detention, nursing home leader, singing, small group leader for women, singles ministry, and Ancient Paths - healing/deliverance ministry. I loved serving and growing in faith as the years passed.

I never thought of ministry as a career option. I grew up in church so serving was a natural thing to do. My ex-husband, years prior, served in Marilyn Hickey Ministries when we lived in Colorado. I learned about the love of the Lord in Orchard Road Church in Littleton, Colorado.

As the years passed, I felt I needed more than I was getting at my local church. Some churches are great for people beginning the journey. I felt I needed a deeper level in giftings and knowledge.

I had these premonitions or sensing's that came and went. I didn't understand why or how I was supposed to manage them. I wasn't getting the answers, knowledge, or experience I needed. Was my experience good, bad, or just weird? I was serving, seeking, praying, and focused, but it wasn't by my will. It was the Lord drawing me closer to experience him.

I'm All In-Lord

Jeremiah 29:11-14

"For I know the plans I have for you,' declares the Lord, 'plans to prosper you and not to harm you, plans to give you hope and a future. Then you will call on me and come and pray to me, and I will listen to you. You will seek me and find me when you seek me with all your heart. I will be found by you,' declares the Lord, 'and will bring you back from captivity…"

I could stop here in telling you what I began in 2009, because this scripture sums it up. I would love to tell you in 2009 I read this scripture and said, "Yes, I am holy," and followed this passage. It didn't happen that way. God had to lead me, but for you, He told me to share this word.

You are special. In 2009, he called me a "forerunner" and put a hunger in me to seek Him through several different methods:

Meditation

- Reading the Bible
- Prayer being a part of the several daily conversations I was having with God
- Sitting quietly with praise music in the background

Removed Distractions

- Absence of cable TV for two or three years (my son was not happy with me).
- Stop talking on the phone so much
- No gossiping
- Not engaging or dating men that lack value to my purpose
- Stop listening to what others needed me to do in ministry and listen for what God needed me to do

My Health

- I opened a Holistic Practice - Total Body Cleanse
- Colon Therapy
- Infrared Sauna

- Foot Detox
- Managed PH levels in my body
- Advanced degree in Holistic Health.

Serving in Multiple Ministries

- Founded Open Heaven Healing Rooms in 2011
- Founded Break the Pattern Project

- The P4 Project for Women - Hyatt Hotel All Night Prayer Meeting
- Leader of the Year at Victory World Church -Community Outreach
- Was a member and in leadership in one church and served in five different church/ministries—Victory World Church, Life Center Church, International House of Prayer, Daystar, and International Association of Healing Rooms—at the same time in healing, prophetic, miracles, and prayer
- Nursing Home Ministry
- Youth Detention
- Women's Detention
- South Africa Missionary work
- Navajo Nation Missionary work

Ministry Training

- Ancient Paths - Lead Facilitator
- Restoring the Foundations - Lead Facilitator
- Prophetic Word Training (four times)
- Miracles Training - Lead Facilitator
- Bethel Sozo Trainer
- International House of Prayer Intern & Staff
- DiSC training
- Ordained International Association of Healing Rooms

As you can see, I uncovered every rock to see and experience Him in His glory in my search for God. I found Him above and beyond my imagination regarding faith, my relationship, and my identity.

God showed me where He was all along in my life. So many times, I'd asked how it was that I knew certain things. I had no one to ask. I wasn't holy nor followed all the rules, so why did I have these gifts? My husband watched from the beginning of our relationship, and he was always confident it was a blessing. I wasn't always sure what to think at times.

In seeking God, I learned He gives gifts, as He wants, to holy and unholy people. This was misunderstood by me growing up in the church. I was getting the training in healing because I was experiencing the power of change over my life that I had to help others get free. God was raising my faith exponentially at such an amazing rate. I was hungry for more.

The Bush That Burns

By 2008, two of my sons were off to college which allowed me extra time to seek out God on my own. It reminds me of Exodus 3 when Moses decided to take a closer look at a burning bush. I had a burning desire that couldn't be quenched by small groups or Sunday church

Let me remind you of Exodus 3. Maybe you have a burning desire to find an understanding of God's purpose for you as a woman made by His hands.

Exodus 3:2-4

"There the angel of the Lord appeared to him in flames of fire from within a bush. Moses saw that though the bush was on fire it did not burn up. So, Moses thought, "I will go over and see this strange sight, why the bush does not burn up. When the Lord saw that he had gone over to look, God called to him from within the bush, 'Moses! Moses!'"

You see, Moses made the decision to go on his own to look at the bush. He didn't ask the others to go with him. He went looking for answers that only God could give him. When God saw Moses seeking an answer, He responded.

I wanted more and felt the Holy Spirit leading me to find it. I started having dreams and words of knowledge I couldn't explain. The experiences were different from the flashbacks of my past. I started knowing things about people when I would meet them or talk to them, and they would ask, "How did you know?"

I would reply, "What do I know?"

They would respond that I had told them something that no one knew about them. I was worried as to why I was having these experiences, and people seasoned in ministry were telling me they hadn't but would show me that it was Biblical. I didn't see myself through God's eyes. I saw myself as unworthy for God to use me in such a unique way.

Ancient Paths

All leaders were advised to go to a course called Ancient Paths at Victory World Church in 2007. I had prayed to God prior, hoping I would get an answer during the training. As I walked in the class, one of the facilitators met me at the door. She said something to me I wasn't familiar with.

She said she had a prophetic word for me. I was open to the experience. She said all the things that had happened to me—my sensing of things and my ability to see into the supernatural—was not an evil thing. She said, "God wanted me to tell you it's been Him all along."

This was life changing for me for two reasons. Since I wasn't a perfect Christian, I feared that if I knew and could see things, then it must be from the devil. My fear was that my prior experiences could also be from the devil. The class was for a weekend. I wept and released key lies I had come to believe about myself.

I had so much doubt that God would talk to me, share things with me. My grandmother loved God, and I never heard her say some of the things I was seeing and hearing. I remember during a break, I went to the church monument on the property, and I heard the Lord so clearly say, "You finally know it's Me in you."

I cried at that spot the whole lunch session. That weekend allowed me a glimpse of my identity in Christ. Was everything that happened to me to prevent this moment?

The Bible

I took it further by praying and asking God to show me how to see and feel Him closer to me. I learned to enjoy the Bible while living in Colorado, but now I became hungry to read the NIV Bible. I couldn't put it down.

The Holy Spirit was leading me to read the word at a high-speed download. It was like sweet candy. I wanted it all. I even took the Bible to the bathroom! It felt like it was being absorbed within me. I saw myself on every page.

The Holy Spirit gave me insight and revelation about my life at a faster pace. I read the whole Bible in two weeks. I was working for myself at the time, so every waking moment and even into the night I was reading.

The Bible had everything. It was so funny, filled with drama, sex, revenge, and victory ... like the best soap opera there was. It was filled with history (which I love), poetry, promises, and Jesus. I was changed after reading the whole Bible for the first time with the Holy Spirit providing commentary.

If you have ever struggled reading the Bible, it's not the Bible ... it's you. You can't get a full revelation if you are not positioned right. After Ancient Paths, the truth included the Holy Spirit with all the power. Have you ever wondered what gifts the Holy Spirit can bring to your life?

I wish I had this when I began. The good news is because I had no traditional knowledge about the Holy Spirit outside of tongues and interpretation, it allowed the Lord Jesus to fill my cup.

Women & Power

Something that I don't believe that is often taught is the positive historical and Biblical relationships between the Father, Son, Holy Spirit, and Woman. Women have done amazing things when allowed in parenting, politics, monarchies, science, education, wartime, civil rights, working conditions, voting, and women's rights.

Maybe it's due to a lack of female leadership, power, and authority within the church that we don't hear sermons about the special relationship women have with God. Women were the bearers of the good news from the cross that Christ had risen from the grave. If it was good then, why isn't it good now?

Women are the volunteers, tithers, and submissive pew holders in the church congregation. It's time that there is more offered than female chat sessions, bake sales, and five-minute motivating messages on getting a husband or keeping one, every spring.

Churches are creating dependent souls, not purposeful, activated women to bring change. Jesus didn't come to sit in the pew. He came to feed and shepherd the lost sheep. The sheep are giving and being entertained, but what about their souls and healing?

Some church leaders are focused on the money and grandiose buildings that can fall or be taken away. Should we place our faith in concrete and marble? Schools are unsafe, crowded, filled with teachers who are overworked and underpaid. Can we create safer schools to educate our children or feed the widows and supplement childcare for single moms?

When love is at that core of what you do, the money will come. As Christian women, we need to evaluate where our money is going and the impact it is having on people who need a savior, the poor, the confused, and the disadvantaged.

I spent many years thinking that if God wanted me to do something, He would share that feeling with someone in leadership. When I think back to my assignments from leadership, it was focused on what they needed, not what God was calling me to do.

Stop waiting for someone to anoint and appoint you. We are all called to save the lost.

You need to gain access to hearing, understanding, and having faith to do things that stretch you out of your comfort zone. How do you know it's God? When you are trying to avoid being stretched in an uncomfortable position or level.

God Declares War

It begins with understanding the early relationship between God and woman. Let's start at the beginning when God declared there would be a war between the Woman and the Devil. Read the whole chapter of Genesis, chapter 3 to understand the situation. You may want to read in multiple versions. Here is the summary in plain terms:

The man blamed the woman because she was deceived by the serpent. The Lord spoke to the woman and asked, "What have you done?" After her explanation, God addressed her enemy first with his judgment in verse 14.

I could write a book just on this topic; when your perceived enemy (like an ex-husband boyfriend, or boss, or children) deceives you, God deals with them first. Don't ever believe they'll get away with the offense against you

Let's get back to Genesis. God tells the serpent that he is cursed and will eat dust forever. Verse 15 is where the war is declared between the serpent and the woman.

This is the verse:

"And I will put enmity between you and the woman and between your offspring and hers; he will crush your head, and you will strike his heel."

What does the word enmity mean? According to Webster, enmity and its synonyms hostility, animosity, and animus all indicate deep-seated dislike or ill will. Enmity suggests true hatred, either overt or concealed.

Since the beginning, women have suffered from lack of knowledge; take this back seat, don't speak, don't think, just look good, say little. Women today are still struggling because we are fighting the wrong enemy with the wrong tools and skills. The enemy is not your spouse, partner, parents, children, or boss. The enemy is the serpent that God spoke to in Genesis, chapter 3. He has been waging war and winning against women.

It's time we war with the truth that God declared in Genesis. He prophesied through the Old Testament of the lamb that would be sacrificed. The sacrifice of Jesus was to come and break the curse that began in the garden against all mankind. God also declared the seed of women would destroy the serpent. I'm here to tell you, life can dump challenging struggles upon you, but you have a promised seed.

Jesus was sacrificed, betrayed, and He took the curse to the cross. Isn't it time women rise knowing that their shame, pain, and wounds are temporary? Tomorrow the sun will shine upon them as victors in the war. Too many women get knocked down and stay down. Your faith, your trust, your identity in Jesus states you will win. You must hold on to the Word as life's bread.

You read it, eat it, believe it, say it until it manifests. I did exactly that with God, and I saw amazing results. I can never go back to the insecure, shameful, controlling, anxious workaholic, striving to prove my worth by my career, house, and things of the past.

You must get this point, ladies ... stop sabotaging your relationships, dreams, and talents by worry and fear. Those obstacles stand between you and your predestined Godly future. Take a stand for your life. Stand with God and His promises. I have been disappointed by man and people too many times to count. When I put it on the line for the word, faith, and belief in God, He never failed me.

This book is about my relationship, my testimony, and that God is for you. If you take this path, your life will never be the same. It's not about the perfect life and money flowing. Life is a constant battle. Jesus came to ensure with the promise of His blood that your struggle can be overcome in this life. I'm not here selling you on eternity.

Some people will tell you to just lay down your life and you will be in Heaven for eternity. No! Jesus already laid down His life for you. He died for you to live prosperously here and in eternity. If it was all about eternity, the Word would say that. Whether you read the Old or New Testament, God's promises are for you today.

Examples of Old & New Testament:

Exodus 14:14

> *The Lord will fight for you.*

Exodus 20:12

> *Honor your father and mother, so*
> *that you may live long in the land the Lord*
> *your God is giving you.*

Isaiah 40:3

> *He gives strength to the weary and increases*
> *the power of the weak.*

Isaiah 41:13

> *"For I am God who takes hold of your*
> *right hand and says to you, do not Fear, I will*
> *help you."*

Isaiah 54:10

> *"Though the mountains be shaken and*
> *the Hills be removed, yet my unfailing love for*
> *you will not be shaken nor my covenant of*
> *peace be removed," says the Lord, who has*
> *compassion on you.*

Isaiah 54:10

> *"No weapon forged against you will prevail,*
> *and you will refute every tongue that accuses you.*
> *This is the heritage of the servants of the Lord,*
> *and this is their vindication from me," declares*
> *the Lord.*

Deuteronomy 31:8

> *"The Lord Himself goes before*
> *you and will be with you; He will never leave*
> *you nor forsake you. Do not be afraid; do not*
> *be discouraged."*

Jeremiah 29:11

> *"For I know the plans I have for you,"*
> *declares the Lord, "plans to prosper you and*
> *not to harm you, plans to give you hope and a*
> *future."*

Psalms 34:17

> *"The righteous cry out, and the Lord*
> *hears them; he delivers them from all their*
> *troubles."*

Psalms 50:15

> *"And call on me in the day of trouble;*

I will deliver you and you will honor me."

New Testament

James 4:7

> *"Submit yourselves, then, to God. Resist*
> *the devil, and he will flee from you."*

1 John 1:9

> *"If we confess our sins, he is faithful and*
> *just and will forgive us our sins and purify us*
> *from all unrighteousness."*

2 Chronicles 7:14

> *"If my people, who are called by*
> *name, will humble themselves and pray and*
> *seek my face and turn from their wicked*
> *ways, then I will hear from heaven, and I will*
> *forgive their sin and heal their land."*

John 3:16

> *"For God so loved the world that he gave*
> *his only Son, that whoever believes in him*
> *shall not perish but have eternal life."*

Mark 11:24

> *"Therefore I tell you, whatever you ask*
> *in prayer believe that you have received it,*
> *and it will be yours."*

I named scriptures above that you can use throughout the weeks to memorize, read commentary about, and meditate on. You may choose other scriptures, as well. The whole Bible is full of God's promise and knowledge for today.

Now, you understand God declared war on the devil because he deceived the woman. I must add Adam and Eve had consequences. God did not desert them. I find it so interesting that what the devil did wasn't against them. It was against God.

You see, Eve was created to be a companion to His Adam. Imagine the jealousy. The serpent didn't go after Eve because she was weaker. He went after

Eve because she was a gift from God to Man. The devil is a thief. He wanted to destroy the gift then and today. She was the perfect companion to ensure Adam's success on earth. The devil wanted to rob, steal, and destroy the greatest gift created for Man.

Battle Zone

1. Share what Genesis 3 means to you personally.

_____

_____

_____

_____

2. Describe how man has treated you versus
   what you were created for.

_____

_____

_____

_____

_____

3. How have you impacted your workplace,
   church, neighborhood, etc.?

_____

_____

_____

_____

4. What needs to change for you to see
   yourself as a gift to the world?

_____

_____

_____

_____

Struggles in Faith

Many people struggle in a relationship with God for many reasons. To be clear, you can't please God without faith.

Hebrews 11:6

"And without faith it is impossible to please God, because anyone who comes to him must believe that he exists and that he rewards those who earnestly seek him."

I don't know about you, but if you have any selfishness in you (which I am sure all of you are too holy for that), the last few words are key. He rewards those who earnestly seek Him. When God speaks, that's a guarantee. Many of you play the lottery and will never win. Here is a sure bet for your life and others.

The first thing we need to get is faith to have a relationship with God. Sounds easy, but wrong. Why do we lack faith in the first place? We have come to believe lies which have resulted in Shame and Fears. Shame and Fears are deep roots. They aren't the only roots, but prevalent with women. In the class, you will explore other roots. In this book, you read about shame and fear which have links to abandonment, abuse, addictions, and rejection.

Relationship with God

The most important part of this book is gaining a relationship with God. I will have to do a separate book to give this subject the justice needed. I am going to share the key nuggets I worked on initially, and throughout the series, you will gain more knowledge of how to grow in faith and in your relationship with God.

God doesn't adhere to our timetable. Our own desires are above our faith and knowledge of God. Where do these desires come from? Other influences, which mean another person's explanation of where you should be.

The struggle is about listening and obeying God. God has our best interests and a specific plan to help you achieve goals you haven't even thought of which can make you a powerful woman with skills and talents beyond your imagination.

How to seek God and find him … I wanted to ensure my belief wasn't based on tradition but on a real relationship and connection with God. The scripture below from Paul talks about the struggle:

Romans 7:14-25 (NLT):

14 So the trouble is not with the law, for it is spiritual and good. The trouble is with me, for I am all too human, a slave to sin. 15 I don't really understand myself, for I want to do what is right, but I don't do it. Instead, I do what I hate. 16 But if I know that what I am doing is wrong, this shows that I agree that the law is good. 17 So I am not the one doing wrong; it is sin living in me that does it.

18 And I know that nothing good lives in me, that is, in my sinful nature. [a] I want to do what is right, but I can't. 19 I want to do what is good, but I don't. I don't want to do what is wrong, but I do it anyway. 20 But if I do what I don't want to do, I am not really the one doing wrong; it is sin living in me that does it.

21 I have discovered this principle of life—that when I want to do what is right, I inevitably do what is wrong. 22 I love God's law with all my heart.23 But there is another power[b] within me that is at war with my mind. This power makes me a slave to the sin that is still within me. 24 Oh, what a miserable person I am! Who will free me from this life that is dominated by sin and death? 25 Thank God! The answer is in Jesus Christ our Lord. So, you see how it is: In my mind I really want to obey God's law, but because of my sinful nature I am a slave to sin.

Verse 23 (NIV):

But I see another law at work in me, waging against the law of my mind and making me a prisoner of the law of sin at work within me.

Imagine this is Paul, who wrote most of the New Testament, inspired of God. I love transparent people who are real. Here, Paul is being frank that he wants to do right, but this flesh, this mouth, makes it challenging.

Battle Zone

1. Name three areas you struggle to do
the right thing in.

_____

_____

_____

_____

_____

2. Can you agree to give the struggle
to Jesus?

_____

_____

_____

_____

3. Do you believe that God is needed
in your daily life?

_____

_____

_____

_____

4. Have you made excuses like, when I
get married, I'll get serious about God?

_____

_____

_____

5.   Do you justify your questionable
behavior by saying everybody else
does it?

_____

_____

_____

_____

_____

The truth of the matter is we all fall in the category of Paul. It's a daily battle to do what's right versus what's quick and desirable. Secondly, you weren't born to be like everybody else.

Women who know me are aware I like to cut to the matter at hand. As women, we talk to anyone who will listen about all that's been done to us. Women rarely discuss how the real struggle and war at hand is in their thinking, emotions, and beliefs about themselves. These beliefs come from a pattern that began long ago. My own pattern of abandonment, fear, and rejection began at an early age. This pattern would plague me for the next thirty years.

The truth of the matter is whether you are a student, in management, business owner, administrative assistant, or stay-at-home mom, we all fall in the category with Paul. It's a daily battle to do what's right.

This book is going to bring you to the path of rest. Are you not tired of wandering around from relationship to relationship, job to job, fussing with husband or kids because of your own hidden pain and insecurities within your heart?

Christian Warrior Women unites you with all women because the struggle is real and against every woman. Your identity brings power and authority that the enemy never wants you to realize. He will use many to strip you of your faith; your parents, teachers, boyfriends, husbands, church leaders, job, children, and friends. So, Christ is who you can trust. He created you. If there is something wrong, He is the one to fix it.

You don't start a relationship with God based on things such as a house, car, a man, or disease. Would you want someone to start a relationship with you based on what they could get? You may be saying, "But I thought that was what I was supposed to do."

The first steps in a relationship:

- Learn who they are, what they believe
- What they want out of a friendship with you?
- Similar interests
- Do you have mutual friends?
- Start spending time together

When I look back at my life now, I can see my one-sided relationship with God's faithfulness, protection, love, justice, and discipline. After seeking God, being healed and facing my fears and insecurities, I understand my relationship as a Daughter in God's Kingdom. Every kingdom has an accepted lifestyle to bring good news and great results for kingdom citizens.

Many people focus their spiritual life with God based on when they get to Heaven. The abundance is for life in the now and forever. Stop with the "woe is me" and get with the "watch my sword squash the head of my enemy."

God's book references your days on earth and in heaven.

People who just let life happen to them as if they are not participants don't understand their identity and the power of God's word. Can you comprehend or understand God's plan for your life? How could my small brain comprehend the thoughts of God who made the sun and moon to shine every day?

The great thing God did, which I totally understand on earth, was make everything reproduce His greatness. Whether plants, vegetables, animals, or humans, we reproduce a seed planted within us. The same God who created the sun, stars, and moon to display each day is the same God that has given us the power to rise each day with the ability to believe, forgive, trust, praise, and raise our faith.

What do you look for in a Relationship?

These are the words I came up with that I look for in a relationship with a friend. I used this matrix to see what I would put under each category with God around these four words: Trust, Honesty, Dependable, Loyal. When I think of all I have been through, God showed Himself to me in these four words.

Think of your life and create your testimonials of His love for you. When the devil comes to remind you of the past, you need to start praising God for what He has done and will do. The enemy will flee at hearing praises of God. Being a Christian Warrior Woman starts with you being Trustworthy, Honest, Dependable, and a Loyal friend. When you make the claim of being a friend, you need to be able to back it up with actions.

Do you know God?

A relationship involves great communication: listening and hearing one another. God already knows my desires and dreams. My ability to hear God came after spending time in prayer, reading His word, meditating, and waiting upon Him. I also acted upon the words I heard God speak.

He doesn't always tell us things we want to hear or act upon. His words to us are precious and require courage. His words have saved my life, others, and offered me to be used to grow the faith of others. Hearing God speak is a priceless experience that I have had the pleasure to have my heart burst with joy several times.

Hearing God

One day, I was driving toward the city of Roswell in Georgia. It was pouring rain. I was on Highway 9, and there were four to five lanes in that section of road. I was driving carefully south on the far-right lane because the rain was coming down in torrents.

While driving, I glanced to the far-left lane on the opposite side of the road. There was a homeless man sitting in a trash can in the pouring rain. As I glanced, I heard the Lord state, "Give the man twenty dollars."

I normally don't carry cash. I was in no position to turn around at that moment. I told myself that if that was the Lord, it would be easier to catch him on the way back because where I was going was the next turn and I had to go north after a quick run in the store.

Then I thought, what a horrible sight, for a man to be so down and out he would choose to sit on trash. Fear tried to creep in with, "You could get carjacked." I decided to believe that if I died because I was being a good Samaritan, God would rejoice with me in heaven.

I made the decision to pull up and offer the twenty dollars and not get out the car. Maybe that was what the Lord told me to do. When I got to the beauty supply store, the store was closed. I laughed because God knew it was closed, and my reason for being there was to give that man the money.

It was still pouring horrendously as I looked for the man sitting in the dumpster. I rolled up next to the dumpster, realizing it was a bus stop, as well. I yelled to the man in the rain. He came to the passenger window and I rolled it down. Rain started to enter the car.

I remembered that I wasn't sure if I had twenty dollars or not because I never carried cash, and I hadn't bothered to check my wallet. The man walked over, and I thought, what am I going to say if I have no money? I opened my wallet and found one twenty-dollar bill.

I said, "Wow, where did you come from?" I was also financially not in a place to give anything away, but disobedience in hearing God was not an option for me. I took the twenty dollars and told him that God had told me to give him the money.

The man took the money, raised it in the air, and started praising God, smiling and showing his gratitude. He leaned in the car, rain still pouring in, and stated he had prayed ten minutes ago to God, asking for the twenty dollars he needed to get on the bus and get food.

He'd said, "God, if You are real, you will cause a miracle. I will serve you, worship you, and believe." He looked at me and continued, "God used you to bring the money." As he continued to praise God, I felt such joy for him but also for myself.

Everytime I hear from God, it feels like the first time. I was filled with joy to watch him praise God in the pouring rain with hand lifted to the heavens. Amid his dirty clothes, homelessness, and despair, he rejoiced. The man then said, "Here is my bus, perfect timing from God."

139

I looked back and saw the city bus coming to where I was parked. I said goodbye, but he was too busy praising God. It wasn't about me with the man. It was about God's faithfulness and the homeless man's faith.

As I drove away I sensed the Spirit state, "Whose faith was greater?"

I said, "The man's faith."

I apologized and stated I wouldn't delay helping someone when the Lord leads.

I ask you:

Have you ever felt led to do something good
that felt strange but blessed someone else?

_____

_____

_____

What hinders you from showing kindness?

_____

_____

_____

What's your thought about homeless people?

_____

_____

_____

How do you help those living in despair?

_____

_____

_____

In my adult life outside of my Mother and husband there has been no one who I could count on when I was challenged financially. God has proven himself to me many times.

I Heard God Speak

Let's begin with when I was living in Littleton, Colorado, in the 90s. I was a single mom with two kids and thinking of adopting another. I was out on medical leave. The leave was turning permanent considering I had no interest in moving to Atlanta, Georgia, with the Coca Cola Company.

Every time I went to the ATL on business, I would hear about horrendous crimes of passion or parents killing kids, on and on. I was currently behind on my taxes, and I didn't have the money. If I didn't pay the taxes, they would sell my home at the courthouse in two days.

My ex-husband was driving me to the hospital to get my incisions checked from surgery. I had been faithfully attending Orchard Road Church where Marilyn Hickey taught and her husband, Pastor Wally Hickey, was senior pastor.

I was so in love with my new truth about Jesus. I gave generously but not because I believed in "you give to get." I gave because after thirty years of learning about the fear of God, I finally understood He loved us and wasn't holding the cross over our heads as a threat.

My ex, Andre, was talking as I was looking out the window, hopeless without any options. Suddenly, Andre's voice went faint, and I felt a presence.

I felt as if I were in a bubble. My eyes starting tearing as I felt a gentleness and peace fill the car. Looking at Andre driving, he obviously didn't sense it because he was still talking. I heard a quiet crystal voice say with clarity, "I love you."

At that moment, I understood everything would be okay. I wasn't thinking about the house at all. I knew I would be okay, whatever happened. The bubble was gone, and Andre said, "You okay?" He could see the tears on my face. I continued to look out the window with a heart full of peace.

Two days later, it was Friday, the day my money to save my house was due. If I had no money, the house would be sold the following Monday morning. I sat in my house, contemplating what to do. A voice came to me and said, "Check your mailbox." Well, when you have debt, the last place you want to go is the mailbox to see more bills you can't pay.

The voice said again, "Go to the mailbox." I put my dog on a leash, and we walked to the mailbox that was down the street from the house. I opened the mail and saw a stack of papers, and a note from the IRS. When a person is down, there's nothing like finding out you owe more.

For some reason, I opened the mail anyway. As I read the note, I was confused because inside was a check and a letter stating I had overpaid my taxes the last ten years and I was due a refund plus interest, which amounted to eight thousand, nine hundred and ninety-nine dollars.

I said to myself, Is the check real? It can't be real. This is a lot of money! I'd known in the car that everything would be all right, but I didn't think like that!

Ephesians 3:20
"Now to him who can do immeasurably more than all we ask or imagine, according to his power that is at work within us."

I called and found out it was real. The small voice had let me know it would be all right in the encounter in my car. I called the courthouse because it was 3:00 pm, and they closed at 4:00. I lived forty-five minutes away. I asked if they would need it cashed first. They stated that they accepted government checks.

I begged them to wait for me. I drove as fast as I could and ran into traffic. I couldn't believe I was within minutes of saving my house, and Friday school traffic was slowing me down. I decided that following the speed limit might not be wise, but I was stuck in traffic, watching the time slip away. When I saw the opportunity in traffic, I took it.

I got to the building with four minutes to go. I raced to the tax and revenue office, and the woman said, "You made it!" I asked her if I was safe. She smiled and said I was. I thanked the Lord.

A few months later, I took a great job and moved north. Can you imagine how God made the IRS give me the money?

Jeremiah 29:11 says, *"For I know the plans I have for you."*

I was in a place of rest in my life with Jesus. He told me He loved me. I believed and trusted Him, never thinking His love was paying for the house. He does this for each of us. He makes a way where there is no way.

I felt so divinely special that day. My family and home were saved. In later years, He would show Himself as my protector repeatedly.

Battle Zone

1. In your group or with another woman,
   ask for someone to stand in faith with
   you about your finances.

   _____

   _____

   _____

   _____

   _____

2. Develop a plan with Jesus to be a
   good steward of the resources. Use
   your mouth to declare you shall have a
   financial breakthrough.

   _____

   _____

   _____

   _____

   _____

3. Be disciplined about spending. Describe
   what you need, not what you want.

   _____

   _____

   _____

   _____

   _____

4. Ask for help, coaching from a reputable source.

Chapter Seven

Gifts Given Freely

There are many books about all the steps and things you must do to be a worthy Christian woman. This book is about how your past journey shall propel you into your future. All those mountains you've climbed and are climbing are your life lessons to overcome and conquer. My journey and message are about how I tried it on my own through many trials, tribulations, disappointments, heartbreak, and life battles.

I learned my many defeats, losses, and wins didn't result in death, but in Christ's faithfulness to me. Even when I didn't trust Him, believe, or depend on Him, He was there paving a way out of nowhere for me. Through this book, my hope and desire are that you understand God's love for you, and women.

I am going to use the article from allaboutgod.com below to provide you with a clear understanding about spiritual gifts. I wish I'd had this when I began. The good news was the gifts of the Spirit made me feel like a child. Every time I witnessed a miracle, it was like the first time.

Gifts of the Spirit - What Are They?

Gifts of the Spirit are special abilities provided by the Holy Spirit to Christians for building up the body of Christ. The list of spiritual gifts in 1 Corinthians 12:8-10 includes wisdom, knowledge, faith, healing, miracles, prophecy, discerning of spirits, speaking in tongues, and interpretation of tongues.

Similar lists appear in *Ephesians 4:7-13 and Romans 12:3-8*. The gifts of the Spirit are simply God enabling believers to do what He has called us to do. In 2 Peter 1:3, it says, "His divine power has given us everything we need for life and godliness through our knowledge of Him who called us by His own glory and goodness." The gifts of the Holy Spirit are part of the "everything we need" to fulfill His purposes for our lives. Our faith activates the strength of the Holy Spirit to release the uniqueness of the seed implanted within each of us.

The key thing is God gives gifts to each person as He decides.

You will see I began by seeking a relationship with God and gained access to be used to display the gifts of the Spirit. I prayed for God to be real, relevant, and personal to me. He has by allowing me to witness and be used to display His glory on the earth today.

The gifts are given to us so that we can be used of God. Most people are unaware of their spiritual gifts, which the enemy is glad that women are defenseless. We can't afford to not wield a weapon in protection of our family, finances, and future. God uses his gifts to edify and grow His people.

As you read through this chapter and the series, ask yourself, "What gift is operating in each scenario?" Start identifying which gifts you have displayed or would like to experience. In your job, you set goals to advance. Why not set prayer and relationship goals to be the willing vessel that God can use? If you could be used to save your family from harm, pray over a sick person and see them healed, or provide a word of knowledge to a generation, would you? Every person has been knitted in the womb of their mother with gifts from God.

I always pray for God's gifts to be displayed in every scenario needed. For example, if someone gets hit by a car, I don't need to prophesy. I need the gift of healing. Many want to be a prophet or a healer, so they can pass out cards with titles like "Prophetess." I smile when I meet people like this because a prophet doesn't need a business card. When she speaks for God, you will know it by her fruit, not her business card.

I spoke at a conference in the Bahamas where the organizer was going to introduce me and wanted to know what title to use. I said, "Just call me Lisa Hawkins."

She said, "No, do you want me to say evangelist, apostle, prophet, or what?"

I answered, "Just Minister Lisa Hawkins."

She looked at me, disappointed, and followed my direction, and that night the congregation was full, and God gave a specific, personal prophetic word to every person. The conference turned from me speaking one time to three times. The Lord poured out miracle healings for barrenness, finances, and emotional healing.

The second night when I was introduced, I laughed because they didn't ask for my title. They had witnessed God display His gift. That night, they read off so many titles I said, "Lord, you have been busy."

It's God that gets the glory, not man or woman. I stand with the title of Jesus and His disciples that my greatest title is Servant. A servant sees everything their master does. I remember sharing the view that I was a servant, and Christian people were like, "You are no servant! God has great plans for you." I realized they didn't get it.

Everything you do in secret with God in worship will be displayed as a gift before man. Just seek Him.

When you simplify the gifts of God, it comes down to love described in 1 Corinthians, chapter 13. You are in Him to be alive because you are holding this book. We all have angels that protect us, guide, and keep us from harm and danger. Did you not know? There are several scriptures in the Bible that discuss this gift.

Whether you have confessed to believe or not, God is protecting you. God's protection is supernatural. Jesus promised we would receive a comforter when He ascended to heaven. The eternal gift is Christ dying on the cross to give me eternal life. Women are a gift. Ah, you shall learn how precious you are. The creation of woman as a gift took creative thinking, and the molding of God.

Battle Zone

1. What gifts are operating in your life now?

_____

_____

_____

_____

_____

2. What gifts would you like God to bless you with?

_____

_____

_____

_____

3. Ask in prayer for a closer relationship with the Lord.
   Seek Him in His scriptures.

The greater gifts come from knowing Him. How do you get to know Him? By reading about Him and His love for you. Shift your life to a new position for God to raise fruit. The gifts will flow from your increase in knowledge about yourself and His word.

Gifts of the Spirit - The Definitions

There is some controversy as to the precise nature of each of the gifts of the Spirit, but here is a list of spiritual gifts and their basic definitions:

- The gift of wisdom is the ability to make decisions and give guidance that is according to God's will.
- The gift of knowledge is the ability to have an in-depth understanding of a spiritual issue or situation.

- The gift of faith is being able to trust God and encourage others to trust God, no matter the circumstances.
- The gift of healing is the miraculous ability to use God's healing power to restore a person who is sick, injured, or suffering.
- The gift of miracles is being able to perform signs and wonders that give authenticity to God's Word and the Gospel message.
- The gift of prophecy is being able to proclaim a message from God.
- The gift of discerning spirits is the ability to determine whether a message, person, or event is truly from God.
- The gift of tongues is the ability to speak in a foreign language that you do not have knowledge of to communicate with someone who speaks that language.
- The gift of interpreting tongues is the ability totranslate the tongues speaking and communicate it back to others in your own language.
- The gift of administration is being able to keep things organized and in accordance with God's principles.
- The gift of help is always having the desire and ability to help others, to do whatever it takes to get a task accomplished.

Gifts of the Spirit - Which One(s) Do I Have?

The Holy Spirit distributes the gifts of the Spirit as He sees fit (1 Corinthians 12:7-11). God does not want us to be ignorant of how He wants us to serve Him. However, it is very easy for us to get caught up in what spiritual gift(s) we have and then only serve God in that area of ministry. That is not how it works.

God calls us to obediently serve Him. He will equip us with whatever gifts of the Spirit we need to accomplish the task or tasks He has called us to. Yes, God calls some to be teachers and gives them the gift of teaching, but that does not excuse the person from serving God in other ways, as well. Is it beneficial to know what spiritual gifts God has given you? Of course, it is. Is it wrong to focus so much on spiritual gifts that we miss other opportunities to serve God? Yes!

There is no magic formula or spiritual gift test that can tell you what gifts of the Spirit you possess. What we need to focus on is faith in God. Do you see a need in your church? Do what you can to meet it. Is there a position in a ministry that is vacant? Pray as to whether God would have you fill it.

If we seek God's will and obey His leading, He will always equip us with whatever gifts of the Spirit we need. Spiritual gift tests can be of some value in determining what areas God has especially gifted you.

As always, though, place far more emphasis on God's Word and submitting to the Lord's leading than you do on the results of a spiritual gift test.

Gifts of the Spirit: What Are the Gifts Used For?

The Apostle Paul indicated that the gifts of the Spirit are equally valid, but not equally valuable. Their value is determined by their worth to the church. In dealing with this matter, he used the analogy of the human body.

All members of the body have functions, Paul declared, but some are more important than others (*1 Corinthians 12:12-26*). The service of each Christian should be in proportion to the gifts which he possesses (*1 Corinthians 12-14*). All believers, as members of the body of Christ, must be serving together for the body to be fully functional.

That is why a church needs pastors, teachers, helpers, servants, administrators, those with great faith, and so on. All the gifts of the Holy Spirit working together are needed to produce the full potential of the church. Since the gifts of the Spirit are gifts of grace, their use must be controlled by the rule of love - the greatest of all the gifts of the Spirit *(1 Corinthians 13)*.

I can tell you, when I get to Heaven, I am going to be accused of stealing other people's gifts. I learned through the Word and the Holy Spirit that the church and believers focus on getting one gift. I grew up in a church that made it seem impossible to have one unless you were the holiest of holy. I bear witness that God wants us to have gifts needed for every circumstance.

My prayer and fasting were to know God. I never prayed and fasted for the gifts. I prayed to know God and see His power in action.

I never said it had to be done by me. I wanted to see a miracle by somebody. I didn't realize I had been seeing miracles my whole life. What about you?

Battle Zone

1. In looking at your own situations,
what gifts of the Spirit have you operated in?

_____

_____

_____

_____

_____

2. You might want to say a prayer of
thanks for God's faithfulness.

_____

_____

_____

_____

I have personally experienced the Holy Spirit use me in many areas at some point in the last ten years. I will share the first public experience I had with interpreting tongues. I was attending a service at International House of Prayer. They were using another location while their building was being built.

I had heard of this IHOP (International House of Prayer) Atlanta, but I thought people were having small group meetings at the pancake house. The Holy Spirit led me to IHOP during my fast. While I was attending service there where I knew nobody, the service went quiet, and this man starting prophesying in tongues. I heard him speaking in tongues, but I could hear him in English.

Then Director Billy Humphrey said, "Let's wait for an interpreter," because the Lord told him there was one present. Humphrey asked again for the person to stand and interpret. I said to myself, If I heard it, surely many others did.

No one stood, so Humphrey asked again. Then in my ear, I heard the voice of the Holy Spirit say, "Will you speak for me?" I wish I could make this sound spiritual for some of you, but at the time I was like, "Are you kidding me? This church is full! Who am I to say a word?"

But, I timidly stood and gave the word, and everybody was praising God while I was like, "What just happened?" I couldn't believe nobody else heard him. In the spirit realm, things happen quickly. My hesitation felt like minutes but was probably one second in the spirit realm.

After service, a man told me I'd given the exact word. If I hadn't spoken, he would have stood. I left feeling encouraged. I had been used of God. At the time, I was just happy to be used and had no clue about titles or gifts I was manifesting. I had experienced God talking to me personally and alone. He had just put me out there. It would be two years later that I would intern, become ordained, and serve on the IHOP team in training, prophecy, and healing.

The Holy Spirit used me in many ways in the years to come. My prayer was for God to give me the gift needed for the specific circumstance to show His glory. If someone is getting divorced, you need the gift of wisdom. My prayer was to witness His glory.

When I would speak to people, they would start telling me the scripture I was talking from. I was just talking, and people could recognize God in my conversation without me quoting or sounding religious. It was a compliment to me because I was just talking. You see, if you fill yourself with good news, it's released.

What gifts were manifested at IHOP?

Spiritual Warning

I am going to share how I came to learn and understand we have angels assigned to each of us, and the Lord is always operating on our behalf. A Warrior Woman defeats her enemies and shares the skills needed to help other women attain victory over the enemy now and in the future.

I was returning from a business trip while living in Denver, Colorado. My kids and ex-husband always picked me up. On the returning flight, I felt struck with the fear and worry. I sensed the plane was about crash. I didn't know what to do.

I looked out the window, and I looked at the flight attendants to see if they looked worried. Everybody was acting normally, but I knew something wasn't right. I looked at the guy next to me. I wanted to scream out and tell someone, but who would believe me? The feeling got stronger, and I felt panicked as to what to do.

I looked at my watch and saw the time 4:07 pm. I thought about my kids coming to the airport and witnessing the plane crashing or hearing about it upon arrival. I started to pray for my kids and Andre that God would help them. I didn't pray for my soul or salvation or anything else.

I felt there was nothing I could do but pray my kids had a good future despite what was about to happen.

I had many premonitions in my life that happened exactly as I saw it. I had no reason to believe a crash was not going to happen. I thought it was better to not make passengers panic. I wondered why I knew. The plane began to land. Everybody was acting like there was no problem.

The plane lowered, lowered, and I thought everything seemed okay. The plane landed, and I was relieved, but didn't understand why I knew a crash was supposed to happen. I was grateful and headed to where my family always picked me up. I'd always told them fifteen minutes earlier than my flight arrived because I hated waiting and my flights often came in early. I was happy to be home and said, "There's a first time for everything. Guess I was wrong on this premonition."

I walked out, anxious to see my sons, but the car was not there. At first, I figured they must be stuck in traffic. They had never been late. Then panic struck me. I said, "No, the accident wasn't my plane!"

I was now overwhelmed and pacing because I didn't know what to do. How could I explain this? Why didn't God warn me it was my children in an accident? Was it to prepare me? Were my children safe? Who would I tell? How would I know?

There were no cell phones (I had one, but individuals didn't have cell phones like that in the 90s). I was flushed and felt faint, weak and in shock. I sat on a bench. Ten minutes went by and no family; twenty minutes went by and no family. I didn't know what to do.

Everything I was working for, striving for, being discriminated against for was to give my children a special, adventurous life. I was lost for words. I looked up the street where the car should come from ... no family in sight. I started wondering if I should just take a cab home. Should I call the police? What should I do now, God?

I looked up the street and saw a minivan ... or at least, I thought it was. Wait. It was my minivan. I stood up and rushed to the curb in case it was one that was the same color. But it was my car. The sliding doors opened, and the kids ran to me yelling, "Mom, Mom, you won't believe what happened to us!" I looked at Andre, and he looked pale and shaken. As I held my kids, Andre began to share what happened.

He stated he was on the interstate driving, and a dump truck loaded with gravel was across the median on the highway going west while they were headed east. The dump truck lost control and came across the median, headed directly for our car. Andre said there was no escape based on the traffic.

He knew they would die; the size of the truck, it being filled with gravel, and the speed it was travelling were too much. Andre said, "I looked at the clock in the van, and the time was 4:07. I knew we would be dead at 4:07 pm."

I was about to pass out because I'd looked at my watch and prayed for them at 4:07 pm. Andre said it was like watching a movie, frame by frame, as the truck came to bring death. He said, "I don't know how it happened, Lisa, but it just missed our car and took out the car behind us." Andre didn't know how they'd escaped, but the people behind them were killed instantly.

I said, "What do you mean?"

He said, "Their bodies are all over the highway, and it is shut down."

The kids and Andre were shaken. I asked, "Andre, tell me again. What time did you say it was when you looked at the clock?"

"It was 4:07, Lisa."

I asked if he was sure.

He said, "Very sure"

I got in the car and loaded my bags. I told Andre what happened to me on the plane. I was happy and felt bad at the same time. My family was saved, but another family was killed. My prayer for them was at 4:07 pm. Did my prayer save their lives? Was God showing me the power of prayer? I was overwhelmed with emotions.

We drove on the opposite side of the highway from where traffic reporters and helicopters were reporting the accident, the fatalities. I could see the bodies covered on the road. I saw the dump truck and realized it could have been me at that scene. I prayed for the family. I was shaken and grateful for my family. My kids were so close to death.

Thanks to God for His tender mercy and loving kindness that saved my family from a horrible death. I am grateful for Jesus alerting me to the harm that led to my praying for my children. There is peace available in Jesus. I don't know the answer as to why the other family lost their lives. I do know I had a relationship with Jesus. I was warned, I prayed, and my family was saved that day. Prayer is significant in your life. Talk to God, for He will talk to you.

Amen.

Battle Zone

1. What gifts was Lisa operating
   during the plane experience?

_____

_____

_____

_____

_____

2. What were the steps that made
   the gifts manifest?

_____

_____

_____

_____

_____

3. Has God saved you from disaster?

_____

_____

_____

_____

_____

How can you hear clearly? I can tell you it starts with:

- Removing the noise
- Declutter and remove worthless hours following somebody else's life in social media
- It includes planning your schedule with Jesus in it

Reading about God in the Bible became an adventure. When I read the Bible, I laugh, I talk to the characters ("Pharaoh, don't do it!"), and I talk to God about what He did in the Bible. God didn't play in the Old Testament.

I know Jesus intercedes on my behalf because I should have been burned up for sins of the past. FYI, not just me, you included, as well. I found worship music that I sat before God with my heart, ears, and soul open to receive. It was Holy Spirit led.

You see, I sat meditating, worshipping, releasing past hurts and pains which brought the light within outward, appropriate for the season. I was honored to be used of God. I wanted to know without a shadow of a doubt that I communicated with Jesus Christ.

I was beginning to realize I was positioning myself by spending time with the Lord. I realized everything that had happened was leading me to this spot. The devil never wanted me to find the truth. He wanted my life filled with disappointment, so I would be distracted from searching for my truth.

Can you see through your mess? Your path looks blocked without an end in sight. I can tell you that vision is based on your flesh and current circumstance. When Jesus is your purpose, you can see past the mess to your victory.

The Best Gift

Don't focus on the gifts. Focus on the gift giver. Too many people walk around with business cards claiming to be somebody. If you are, you don't need business cards. The Lord's presence announces you every time your mouth opens.

Christians caught up in titles are no different than the world. Every time I attended a service where someone claimed to be something, I left disappointed. Then God shared the secret: if they must tell you their gift, they don't have it.

The gifts of God come with a weight. When you look at someone and know that they are headed for destruction, it's painful when you can't convince them to change. I have worked with many women who God has shown me their potential. They were too lazy, unforgiving, critical, sabotaging, and insecure to fulfill it.

The devil had them occupied with false responsibility and worldly goals unaccomplished. It didn't matter how many prophetic words were shared, tears shed, prayers prayed, or even walking it out with them. It was easy for me to recognize it because I had also been a victim of lies and deceit from the devil.

How do you get gifts from God? A relationship with God and Jesus leads to gifts from the Holy Spirit. What is your relationship with God? If you are unsure, a good place to start is in repentance of being unsure. A relationship with God begins with making a choice to cast your cares and raise faith in Christ for all things.

Take Back and Stoke the Gift(s)

If you're aware of the gifts you have, declare it! Say it out loud in thankfulness. If you are not sure, wait on the Lord Jesus. He will use you when you least expect it.

Chapter Eight

Identity

<

John 15:5

"I am the vine, you are the branches. If you remain in me and I in you, you will bear much fruit; apart from me you can do nothing."

I f you believe in God, what's your identity? What does the Bible say about believers?

http://www.biblestudytools.com/topical-verses/bible-verses-about-our-identity-in-christ

John 1:12

"Yet to all who did receive him, to those who believed in his name, he gave the right to become children of God - children born not of natural descent, nor of human decision or husband's will, but born of God."

Ephesians 1:5

"He predestined us for adoption to sonship through Jesus Christ, in accordance with his pleasure and will."

Read Ephesian, Chapter 1.

After you review the scriptures and think about them, you should make a choice. You have been predestined to receive daughter ship and the fullness that Christ represents based on faith which states He has power over every authority (Colossians 2:9), power over all authority meaning good and evil.

If my identity is based on my experiences, environment, and beliefs, I can choose my identity. You don't have to be stuck with a label from an alcoholic dad or a bitter mother who lacks vision for your life. You are not trapped in poverty or despair. You can decide to accept the identity that God gives you in His word. Don't let molestation, divorce, singleness, shame, or rejection be your identity. Every day, we meet people who think you don't see, hear, or feel their identity, but we do. It comes out of their mouths and through their behavior.

When people hear you talk, who would they identify you with?

If someone watched your behavior, what would they identify you with?

Ask someone at your job or a close friend. See if they give you behaviors, works, or things in their answer.

Loneliness is not your identity. We serve a God that supports our major and minor insecurities, struggles, and despair. Resist the devil, and he will flee. When he flees, wait for the Lord to respond to you.

Dancing with Jesus

It was almost midnight, New Year's Day (New Year's Eve is a huge holiday for me personally). Of all the holidays, not having Mr. Right on New Year's Day was a little depressing for me.

I sat on the California King bed, and I looked at the other side and realized I wasn't alone. A voice said to me, "Stop looking over here at this empty bed. Make a phone call, text somebody. You know men who would like to be here. You are a beautiful woman. You do not deserve to be lonely. How long do you think you can keep this up? You were not made like those boring church girls. If He loves you, He will forgive you. What about Grace??? Men in your own church have told you that. You have options…"

This went on until…

The Holy Spirit within me spoke back in tongues, and the demon left. I turned back to turn off the light. Suddenly, the room was illuminated with the blue light from my TiVo box. The room looked like a nightclub with lights. I heard a beautiful, still voice ask me to dance with him.

I looked up, and his hand was stretched to me, bidding me to come. I immediately realized I was naked and thought I should have worn pajamas. As I took his hand, he took my memory back to a list of things I'd wanted to accomplish after college.

There was only one item left: to ballroom dance with my one true "LOVE." Recently, during fasting, I'd had one more request. I wanted to know that I had personally been in the presence of God. I'd envied Moses and others that saw and felt Him near. I wanted an Old Testament experience.

He asked me again, "Will you dance with me?"

I took his hand, and a song from my iPod started to play, Josh Groban's "To Where You Are." He told me the words in the song were the message He'd heard from me to Him. He knew I loved him. He knew this day was difficult for me.

We started dancing a waltz type of dance. He swirled me around the room. I had never danced like that before in my life. I felt such love, peace, and joy. I thought my heart would burst with the feeling. He told me that he loved me like no other. He had given me a rare ability to love passionately. He wanted me to stop asking him to take it away. "Be the girl you were before your father died," He told me.

I will use your beauty as an example. He said, "I adore you." We swirled, and the room felt like it had no limits. The same song played over and over. He glided me around the room, and I felt the presence of others cheering us on. There were heavenly beings expressing happiness at watching us dance. I danced like a professional before the Lord. He told me, "We will dance again. I will come back for you."

I didn't want the moment to end. I said, "Please stay with me."

He said, He would. I replied, "No, like this."

He said, "I can't." He said we would dance again. I started to cry. I didn't want the love to stop. He said, "one day, you will feel this again, and that man is the one for you. You can never settle."

I remembered the Lord spoke to me prior that what He had planned for me could only happen when I was covered. I would be in danger and need the prayer of that man who would provide the covering.

You are probably thinking this was a dream...

They were all gone, and I was left with the blue light. I was on the floor at the foot of my bed, crying. It couldn't be over. I asked myself if it was a dream. It was just five minutes, but how did I get from the bed to the floor in a position like I had lowered for royalty?

I scrambled for my cell phone to check the time. It was 3:15 am. But, I had gone to bed five minutes ago! The Holy Spirit said, "You were dancing with the Lord for three hours." I tried to dance again by myself. I couldn't move gracefully. I felt the carpet. I asked Him to come back. I cried because I wanted to know why He had left me here. I knew that He would be the "only true LOVE" I would ever have.

I was desperate to feel Him close. I laid in the bed to savor the moment and fell asleep. When I arose, I felt refreshed with a whole new feeling of how to express myself. Within a week, I enrolled in ballroom dancing and felt such a rush.

I knew the dance was a type of waltz. When I started taking dancing lessons, it felt nothing like the night I'd danced with my King. My feet were wrong, and my body was not gliding. I remembered He'd said, "Be the girl you were before your father died."

I worked hard and loved ballroom. During a lesson, my partner said, "Stop leading. I'm the man; let me lead you. Even if you know the move, let me put you there."

The Holy Spirit came in the room and spoke to me and said, "You are here to be an example and to learn how to be led. Let him lead you."

A month after dancing, all my male dance partners started complimenting me on how well I was following. They also joked how in my first month, it was a battle. Three months later, I was asked to compete in a competition in Atlanta. Most people wait years to compete.

I told them that it was too expensive and that the Lord would have to give me a sign. He did. The competition was on my birthday. Then He told me to give it to myself as a gift.

I competed in smooth rhythm. We were in the final heat of three dancers, and I had to dance a Viennese Waltz again. I was exhausted because I had already danced eight times in a row.

My partner said, "Lisa, you can do this." We started the dance. He said, "Lisa, keep your arms up, or they will know you're tired." I agreed, and a bright light burst in front of and around me. It felt like the warmth of the sun, and my partner was gone. The spirit gave me energy and said, "I am here."

I floated, I glided, my feet moved without any thought or effort from me. I didn't want it to stop. I heard people cheering and calling my name in the far off. I remembered I had danced this dance before. The Lord and I danced the Viennese Waltz together. I was wowed. Then the music stopped, the dance ended. I didn't want it to end.

My dance partner said, "Wow, you were great! I never saw you out there. I thought I was dancing with an angel."

I told him it wasn't me. He had to take my hand to get me off the competition floor. I smiled and laughed because the Lord said He would dance with me again. I thought He meant in heaven. The Viennese Waltz is the dance I shared with Jesus.

People from my dance studio and the owner came and said they had never seen me dance like that. They said I looked like royalty and even Michelle Obama could learn a thing or two. I laughed and said, "I am a child of a King!"

During the competition on that day, I won five awards. Total competition, I won eight. The Lord danced with me on Day One. I got an award for Viennese Waltz!!!!

This story was written to share how the Holy Spirit can fill that loneliness. It can work in your life and inspire you to do things you never thought possible.

I am still dancing and preparing with a passion for the main dance in heaven one day. Remember, He is always there! Our goal is to get to "where He is," as the songs states. The words of the song say it all.

God Bless You!

Lost Identity

I think most people believe they know their identity. I would disagree. If Christian women knew their identity, our families, our homes, our careers, our relationships with God, men, and work would be the envy of everyone we met. You can't dream big enough if you don't know the identity God gave you.

God is the one who gives you the ideas you believe are too impossible to accomplish. It will never come from a person. Most women are not going to tell you that you are the smartest, brightest woman they've ever met. If you know who you are, then you know who you are not in troubling situations. You don't allow yourself to be a victim or dwell on the past.

You realize bumps in the road are temporary. Why is it so easy for women to believe that bad things will happen or in what they will never have?

Stop letting people or social media give you identities that you were not born to fulfill. Warriors know how to spot a traitor. If the people around you keep telling you what you can't do, they don't know God, which means they don't know you. Drop these people fast and find a friend who builds your self-esteem.

Create your own plan and playbook from God. A bold and powerful woman knows she can do all things with Christ. How do I know? Philippian 4:13 tells me through Christ, it's possible. State that at work, in a relationship, and when you fail miserably. You must gain insight from God. Don't quit. The devil tells you it's too hard to be good. I don't want you to be good. I want you to be great.

All of us have been on a job interview where we've told people all the things they wanted to hear about how hard we work, how smart we work, how well we work with others. The interviewer rarely asks the deep questions like, "What would make you quit?" or "Describe your identity?"

What would you say? Take a moment and think how you would answer.

I Am a W-O-M-A-N

There was a commercial in the 80s with a woman who stated she could work, fry it up in a pan, and never let her husband forget he is a man. I may have to turn in my women's liberation card after this statement, but working and dealing with corporate politics, taking care of the kids' needs emotionally, physically, spiritually, and all their activities, and paying all the bills is not easy. Women need to stop talking the foolishness that single parenting is a good thing. I did it for twenty years after my divorce. It can be stressful and challenging even if you have money if you don't.

The gender lines are blurred in the world but not with God. Today women are wearing too many hats and not happy in many of them. Whether married or single, women are exhausted and overworked. The divorce rate is at almost fifty percent, and women eagerly push to brag on how they can handle it all. I was one of those women.

I have worn many hats as a top executive, breaking gender/racial barriers in corporate America, a wife, and mother serving my community, serving in church, attending sporting events with kids, chauffeuring kids, the housekeeper, the planner, the cook, and the hostess. I could name more, but you get my point. I am for equal pay and equal opportunity, but I like a man to open the door for me (thank you).

As women, we need to stop comparing and watching reality shows that are far from reality and read your manufacturer's notes. This isn't about going backward. It's about going forward with a plan and a vision for your life no matter what your status, socioeconomics, race, or ethnicity. In 2018, it's shocking to see women allowing themselves to be dishonored to deal with loneliness. I never want to be so lonely that I give up my self-respect to someone unworthy of my companionship.

You must be proactive in healing your soul and uncovering the lies you have come to believe and allow the truth to set you free. As a woman, you hold the fate of future generations. no matter how low you have fallen, God is there. The exercises allow you to hear God for yourself.

Most churches or groups tell you that attending their church each Sunday will bring you closer to God. It's what you do seven days a week that draws you to God. Jesus didn't come to establish a religion of denominations where most disagree on style of worship. Jesus came to break the curse and bring freedom and eternal life.

As a Christian Woman, I want to facilitate bringing the true ammunition to the battlefield for women to wage war confidently—for your life and your children's lives and generations to come.

Can you imagine today that you can have the keys to unlock the chains to the minds of your children? How do I know? This journey humbled me before God in the privacy of my life. I attended church and fellowshipped with other believers. The real work happened the other six days I chased God.

This book is for women tired of trying to win in their own confidence. It's for the person who realizes she can no longer continue the path she's headed. It's not a hand holding program. It's called Warrior Women because you must fight and want this more than buying the book. Many people own tons of books they never read.

Your identity is in Christ who lives within you. You have all the answers to your life within. Your identity has been waiting for you to hit the "on" switch.

This plan is for you by God to change your life now. Now is the time to look in the mirror and say, "I cast out all the confusion, shame, anger, bitterness to the pit of hell." State, "No longer will I let the enemy attack me and my family. I can take back my life and trust God to win my future and the war."

Fight for Your Identity

No matter what your religion, occupation, gender, or nationality, understanding your identity is the key to your success. Your occupation is not your identity. For most of my life, my identity was my career achievements. Breaking barriers for equal pay, racism, sexism was at the heart of my battle in every position I held.

When my position at PepsiCo became unbearable, I felt lost as to where I would go from that experience. It never hit me that my whole life and soul were based on what I did. That was the true revelation. My pain in that company came from my lack of identity. I should have sued them the first time it was said and move on. I am smiling at myself as I type the last sentence.

Fantasy Identity

I also had my identity tied to the love of my life. When that ended, I couldn't imagine my life without him. I learned painfully my identity wasn't in the job nor in another human being. I had my identity tied to a company that could fire or lay me off at any minute. I had my identity tied to a man who could leave, die, or fall out of love with me.

What identity should I Fight for?

What you believe about yourself determines if you fulfill your identity. In our society women are speaking, protesting, and exposing the wrongful treatment of women. Whether its wages, shattering the glass ceiling, or male/female relationships, women feel they are being discriminated against or not fully appreciated. What's sad is women feel the same way in ministry and in the church. We have come a long way if you look at the number of women running nations and multinational corporations, but we are far from equal pay and opportunity in the boardroom.

From Genesis, a woman's identity was declared as victorious, but man added his interpretation and women began going backward instead of forward. I applaud women who speak out against injustice and demand their equal rights. I never competed against women in the workplace. I was always out to prove I was better or equal to a man. To get noticed, you must prove you are better than men. As a minority female ... well, I had double to prove.

Prior to healing, I saw my total identity as being a woman who was:

- The first female in every job in top corporations
- Worked hard to be number one
- Competitive
- Open to new experiences

- Risk taker
- Loyal
- Wanted to give my kids a dream life
- Don't mess with me because I was revengeful

My spiritual identity was:

- Be a generous giver of funds
- Serve or volunteer
- Tither in bullets
- Support those God has called
- God can't use me for anything significant, so, I will be a great giver.

For the last thirty years, I had many top nationally known evangelists or ministers pray or give me personal prophetic words one on one. I let them go in one ear and out the next because I had my identity. I am sure you have had many people tell you positive things about your capability that you blew off, as well. TD Jakes, Joyce Meyers, Marilyn Hickey, and more prophesied I would be doing what I am doing with this book many years ago.

I saw myself climbing the corporate ladder and making a spot for women in a male dominated industry. That was my purpose and determination. I had developed a false concept of myself even though to the world I was successful.

According to study.com the definition of personal identity is the concept you develop about yourself that evolves over the course of your life. This may include aspects of your life that you have no control over, such as where you grew up, or the color of your skin, as well as choices you make in life, such as how you spend your time and what you believe. You demonstrate portions of your personal identity outwardly through what you wear and how you interact with other people.

This definition may remind you of where you are now. Here are some personal identity factors that affect your perception of yourself:

- Victim of Rape, incest
- Physical abuse
- Prison

- Homeless
- Abandoned, rejected
- Hunger, starvation
- Poverty
- Racism
- Divorce
- Single, never married
- Barren
- Lesbian
- Abortion
- Murder

Some of these are just circumstances you could be born into that could make life very challenging. The good news is that even through your darkest days, God knitted his talent, plan, and purpose in you. You can make the choice like Mary Magdalene did. Let them demons go and follow Jesus.

Her identity changed for all time to be the bearer of the good news from Christ. You too can be that woman because of the resurrection. Jesus used Mary Magdalene to see, witness and proclaim He was risen. She had seven demons cast out of her before she could see, witness, and bear witness.

If you read this definition, it would sound like identity grows in time. We were born with an identity after the doctor slapped our butt, and when we cry, it begins. Our personal identity influences our future, but we must make the choice to either accept the world's definition or God's. God didn't make you a second-class citizen. You must close your ears to the lies and stereotypes. Earlier, I referenced many people who told me who I was according to their world view, but there was an internal compass showing me a different view.

What God has knitted in your inner spirit needs to be released (Psalms 139:13). I had a blind faith in myself. I had a confidence in myself, not necessarily God. This was my way of controlling who and what I would become. I had the "Me" spirit going on due to not trusting anybody with my future.

Identity is a choice, not a circumstance. What you choose to believe that matches God's word is the beginning of understanding your identity. When you start claiming that you are the way you are because of somebody else, you are talking about your personal identity. I want you to realize you have a personal and spiritual identity. I was living my personal identity hard and fast until I surrendered to what I chose to believe.

As you see in the above, your identity includes what you choose to believe and spend your time doing. These are choices. It also references your outward behavior and choices you make in life. I teach Christian Warrior Women that their identities are given to them by God. You must make the choice to accept your God-given identity by accepting your creator and Jesus who died for you to have the power, authority, and endless capacity for success.

Battle Zone

1. What do you believe about your
    personal identity?

_____

_____

_____

_____

_____

2. What do you believe you can change to
    improve your personal identity?

_____

_____

_____

_____

3. What do you believe about your spiritual
    identity?

_____

_____

_____

_____

_____

4. Where do you spend your time?

_____

_____

_____

_____

5.   What areas are wasting your time?

_____

_____

_____

_____

_____

6.   What do you believe is knitted in you
for success?

_____

_____

_____

_____

_____

7.   What personal identity characteristics
are stifling your spiritual identity?

_____

_____

_____

_____

Chapter Nine

Ancestral Patterns

Exodus 20:12

"Honor your father and your mother so that you may live long in the land the Lord your God is giving you."

Generational Blessing *Psalms 112:2*

"Their children will be mighty in the land; the generation of the upright will be blessed."

Generational Baggage *Exodus 20:4-6*

"You shall have no other gods before me. You shall not make for yourself an image in the form of anything in heaven above or on earth beneath or in the waters below. You shall not bow down to them or worship them; for I, the Lord your God, am a jealous God, punishing the children for the sin of the parents to the third and fourth generation of those who hate me, but showing love to a thousand generations of those who love me and keep my commandments."

Many women state they love the Lord, but my question to you is: do you keep His commandments? Women would not be in such a desperate state to trade their virtue for a man, career, money, and new body parts if they were keeping God's commandments.

Ancestral Blessings

Many ministries talk about generational curses, but I want to share the good news of ancestral or generational blessings. Every family has talents and gifts that are recognizable amongst family members. The range is wide and should be appreciated, celebrated, passed on and praised for the blessings from Jesus. Think of your parents, siblings, grandparents, aunts and uncles ... what's the blessing that flows through your ancestors?

It could be:

- Great health
- Intelligence
- Faith
- Creative talents - music, dance, art, song
- Financially secure - property owners
- Marriage - all children born in marriage
- Prayer warriors
- Sound mind

Make a list of three of your ancestral blessings that have been passed down to you:

1. _____
2. _____
3. _____

Do you praise God for your blessings? Do you pray that your children will respect and use the family blessings for their success? God knitted us in our mother's womb and gave us blessings from our generational line. Do you have pride about your family? There are no perfect families. Every family has junk in the trunk if you look deep enough.

Jesus Shares Ancestral Roots

Maybe you don't know your history due to foster care or adoption. Don't be dismayed; the Lord does like sharing secrets! Many times, we think of talking to God about major issues, but if we have ears to hear he will share the secrets of life that can shift your family's future into enlightenment and joy. All our challenges are minor to God, but a breakthrough for us.

Let's Find Your Ancestral Roots

Everyone is in search of their roots, as well as what percentage of this race and that race we have within us. It sounds exciting if you are living in a country that values the cultural melting pot. When it's all said and done, we are all multicultural. We are all related. Everything you don't like in another race of people, you have in your own race.

I was shocked when I reviewed my DNA and learned from as far north as Norway and East to West Africa, God made me from a strong and mighty people. Why are they mighty? Because my generational blessing is from people who love God, and Psalms 112:2 states their children shall be mighty.

Loving the Lord didn't mean they didn't mess up a lot. They were very human and flawed as I am. There is another identity statement for us to use. Not only am I a warrior, but a Mighty Warrior Woman. Maybe you are too, based on ancestral roots. Amen!

What are your ancestral roots? The ancestral root is the door the devil uses to enter every generation of your family.

Many people understand generational roots when it comes to health, or emotional addictive roots such as:

- Health Roots
- Cancer
- High blood pressure
- Diabetes
- Addictions run in the family
- Addictive Roots

- Substance abuse
- Physical abuse
- Sexual abuse

The health and addictive roots are in the physical, meaning they can be seen, but the generational root can't always be seen because it's in the spiritual. Roots are hidden deep below the surface of the pretty face, great body or smarts. The roots are in the heart, pumping the messages to the brain for a reaction.

A person who is an alcoholic can be seen because they drink excessively. You may notice they are not in control of their faculties. Why, or what, makes them drink is the spiritual root we can't see.

Many programs for people who have the disease of addiction focus on them acknowledging who they are as an addict all the time after years of being free. It also appears they are set up to be always an addict.

In my opinion, that doesn't line up with the Word. When the Lord healed, or the apostles healed, they never told folks to continue to claim their sickness or sin. The Lord said, "Pick up your mat and walk." When we accept Christ, the word says we are a new creature. We were born in sin, and every day we are tempted to sin. But one day, I decided to become a child of God. Therefore, I am no longer bound to a life of sin.

Christ began a new life in you. Read 2 Corinthians 5:17. When you trusted Christ to be your Savior and Lord, you began a new spiritual life. God will increasingly produce many new qualities in you as you respond to Him.

These new qualities are not your past. Generational roots of pain and shame are broken. The root is what led someone to, or caused, the drinking, drugging in the first place. Was it shame, rejection, unforgiveness, abandonment, depression (about what), loss?

You must seek out the root cause, not the manifestation of picking up the bottle, pornography or cutting, shooting/snorting up. What pain are you trying to escape from? Once identified, you can develop a key response strategy.

I have found in healing sessions that years of therapy turned into weeks in discovering with God their roots that have affected them and their family line for generations. After identification, healing takes time, but so does your relationship and knowledge of God.

Isn't it time you focus on passing the blessings of a thousand generations through Jesus? Has your family experienced enough pain for you to be chosen by God to bring the light into a dark place in your family history? A Warrior Woman is that fire starter needed to burn out the old and make everything new in Jesus' name.

Jesus Finds Lost Ancestral Roots

My husband was a foster child his whole life. He had no clue about his birth family. His birth certificate was filled with fake information. He was left at an orphanage and would never know about his biological family.

We met in college at Syracuse University where he was a starting center and a known beast basketball player in the Big East in the 80s. Within the first few weeks of our relationship, a person contacted him, stating that he was a birth relative and wanting to bring his birth mother to meet him. I was so excited for him because this was a chance for him to get information he never knew.

When I called to learn of how the reunion went, he explained that someone had pulled a prank. I went up to see him the following weekend. I could feel in my spirit the sense of deep hurt and woundedness that this situation created. I felt so bad for being overjoyed and enthusiastic about the opportunity.

I remember that this was the moment that probably sealed our future and later marriage, and I was unaware. I looked at him and said, "How horrible this is, and how very sorry that a person could be this hurtful!" Maybe somebody did it to mess with his head before a basketball game. When I held him, I said in the deepest part of my soul I will find his mother. I had no clue of how or where to start. I declared it with a confidence that I knew somebody had to make this happen. I decided it would be me.

I tried to look for her on my own back in the days when we had 411 operators. Social services told me the government could not find her. They told me it was hopeless due to the birth certificate containing fake information. For whatever reason, I still felt something was true on the birth certificate.

A couple of years went by after we married, and I was still hitting dead ends everywhere. I didn't tell my husband I was searching because I didn't want to get his hopes up again. After we had our son, I had a dream. In the dream, a voice told me his birth mother is in a state, in a city I had traveled to and was familiar with.

I don't know about you, but I was like, "Lord, can't you just give me the city?" I narrowed my search to Texas, Tennessee, North Carolina, New York, and New Jersey. I found nothing in Texas, and nothing in New York.

I had another dream years later when my husband and I divorced, and my son was three-year-old. I had still been looking and praying for answers for my own son, as well. In that dream, I sensed I must look for her that day and in that moment. I decided to call the cities in Tennessee I was familiar with: Memphis, Cleveland, and Chattanooga.

The short of the story is I found his mother that day through a random call to a stranger who remembered a classmate that left Chattanooga for New York in the 60s and the grandmother still lived in Chattanooga. That day I spoke to my ex-husband's grandmother and received a call from his birth mother.

His birth mother's first reaction was, "What are you?" She told me she falsified every piece of paperwork to insure she would never be found. Her first question was: did I seek the help of a psychic? I told her God told me.

The family reunion with his mother was far from what I'd hoped for. I will never forget the day I told my ex-husband I found his mother and family. To this day, it was the first amazing moment God helped me shape and witness a person finding their ancestral roots. His siblings looked just like him and welcomed him with love and warmth.

The Lord helping me find his birth family led to other siblings that had been put up for adoption. My son now had family on both sides of the family.

God believes in family ties. You must believe in family ties. Your confidence, your insecurity, your marriage, your children, your finances could be linked to an ancestral root of blessing or curses. Knowledge is power. Use wisdom, prayer, and trust, and He will lead you to understanding when there is no one to fill the gap.

Battle Zone

1. Do you like to uncover mysteries about family history?

_____

_____

_____

_____

_____

2. Are there secrets in your family that no one talks about?

_____

_____

_____

_____

_____

3. Are there children born outside your parents' marriage that you don't know or blame?

_____

_____

_____

_____

_____

4. What steps can you take to embrace all
    your ancestral roots, good and bad?

_____

_____

_____

_____

_____

5. Ask the older members in the family
    about your history prior to paying a
    service for your bloodline.

_____

_____

_____

_____

_____

My Father's Ancestral Blessing

When I was a child prior to his stroke, my dada prayed over me that we would always be connected in this life when anything good or bad happened. In the hospital, he tried to remind me it was our family's gift. I tried to get him to stop talking because he appeared uncomfortable. His words were true. I had no confidence in some special gifts or talents from God at the time.

He looked at me and said, "It will grow stronger, and you won't be able to deny it. You already have sensed your gift." The truth was I had felt premonitions. Without going through all the details here, when my father died, I knew before the phone call ever came.

I was asleep when my father died. He came to me in a dream, and he was happy, free and grateful he could say goodbye to me. I said, "Daddy, don't leave me, come back." He said, "I must go, but I had to say goodbye to you." It was a beautiful moment to experience.

I woke up crying and calling for my mother. She tried to tell me it was a bad dream. I said, "No, he was there, he was leaving, he is gone. I can feel it." I begged for Andre and my mother to believe me. My husband was trying to calm me at the time the phone rang. The call was from the hospital. My father had died.

As I let go of the phone, I heard the words he had spoken to me as a child: "We will be linked until I die. You will always know if I'm in danger as I will know, as well." His words had proven true in life and now in death. All my husband, Andre, could say was how sorry he was, but what a wonderful thing he'd said goodbye.

My dad never said a negative word to me my whole life. He encouraged me, and never let me buy into sexism or racial divide. He wanted me to be a lawyer. He thought I was the smartest person and capable of anything I put my mind to. My father's best advice was, "If you want to be smart, hang with smart people; if you want to be rich, hang with rich people." He told me my place was not with poor, hopeless people. His words are so true.

When you want to be healed of stinking thinking, you can't hang with other stinking thinking people. If you are depressed, get away from other depressed people. I would later live by the motto, "If you want to be successful, learn from successful people."

What spiritual gift brings answers in dreams?

My Grandmother

Have you ever realized the prayers of the past and present are hanging over you each day? Many people may not come from a family that prays over the generations and family members. You can be the woman that stands in the gap for her children, grandchildren, and generations to come.

I know that my relationship with God began with the generational blessings and fervent prayers of a woman with a seventh-grade education. Born in 1910 on a remote island in the Bahamas, she had hopes, dreams, and trust in God. When my grandmother passed in 2005, I felt the shift in responsibility to pray for my family and children. All my antics and selfish living prior was covered by my grandmother's prayer. I was given the grace and mercy to know it was time for me to cover my own family in prayer.

Battle Zone

1. Who are the prayer warriors in your family?

_____

_____

_____

_____

2. Who are the family members who have the strongest faith, trust, and belief in Jesus?

_____

_____

_____

_____

3. Has their faith affected you? Are you stifling your generational blessing?

_____

_____

_____

_____

4. Have dreams ever brought answers to tough decisions?

_____

_____

_____

_____

_____

5.   Share how dreams have helped your life.
     How did you know to trust the dream?

_____

_____

_____

_____

_____

Speak Ancestral Lessons

Step one:

Take time to learn ancestral history

Step two:

Focus on the positive ancestral patterns

Step three:

Use your tongue to speak life

Step four:

Prayer over family, children

Step five:

Activate your faith

Step six:

Praise God

Step seven:

Trust God

When tough times come, start declaring the ancestral blessings over yourself and your children.

Focus on the positive.

Use your tongue to speak out loud the power that breaks the yoke. Pray over your children daily, declare your seed shall be blessed (even during crazy times). Use scriptures over your children, husband, and others brought to you by God to pray for. Activate your faith in the ancestral giftings and talents. Praise God that you have the chance to bless a thousand generations.

Ancestral Roots

Family life can be stressful, loving, and painful all at the same time, but you only get one family. All joking aside, when you are seeking healing, your family is a great place to start. As I've discussed throughout the book, my early years laid a foundation for insecurities that lasted many years. During the healing process, I learned about my generational roots, blessings, and curses.

I could see the patterns in my family that I allowed in by opening the door of sin. There is a lot of debate about generational curses, but it comes down to one thing: if you have sin, you have curses. The curses that attach themselves to us are the curses that the devil has been attacking your family with. Whether your generational attack is emotional or physical, sin brings a pattern that you can either accept or refuse.

Personal Roots

Personal roots are the sins you have committed to continue the generational roots, and some you may have added to the line in your lifetime. Example: if children born out of wedlock are in your generational roots, you may have continued the behavior by having children out of wedlock. You may have added additional sins by having an abortion, affair with a married person, cutting yourself, selling drugs, embezzlement, murder, hate, racism. These may be new personal sins that you are adding to the future generations. Let's stop the madness with a prayer right now.

Lord, Father in Heaven, I repent for repeating the ancestral patterns of sins. Lord, I cast off and break agreement with the sinful roots of _____, _____, *and* _____.

Lord, I am cleansed and a new creature because Christ died and took the curse to the cross. I am no longer bound to any ancestral patterns of sins, vows, pledges, or blood oaths made on my behalf. I am filled with the glory and grace of God to live and walk out a higher calling to bless future generations for a thousand years.

Adoption Changes Ancestral Roots

Maybe the war against me was to prevent bringing change to a generational pattern in my son's life. Saving an African American male child out of the foster care system came with a battle of life and death. I had no idea what I was really at war against during the adoption process. God used me to break him free of the bondage that had robbed and stolen the identity of his family members.

While I was in the adoption process, I lost my job. Then, as if that wasn't enough, my home burned down. When I told the social worker that I may have to stop the adoption process, she told me that based on my home study and my life, she had no doubt I would land on my feet.

My mother and others said, "You can't adopt while unemployed, that's crazy!" I was a single mom and didn't need the additional stress and responsibility.

I prayed to God, never thinking the distractions were to prevent the adoption. I told the Lord I would step out on faith because there was a child who needed me to break the pattern for his future.

I felt in my heart the Lord's confirmation that this was my son. I was living in a hotel with all my personal items destroyed in a fire and no job. It had to be God because in my rational thinking, who adopts a son during this time of loss? One week after my son arrived to live with us permanently, I got a call about a job in Denver, Colorado. Within a month, my family was moved from our hotel to a beautiful city called Highlands Ranch, Colorado.

Breaking an ancestral pattern can be painful, but when you overcome and snuff out your enemy, the spoils are unbelievable. To this day, living in Denver was one of my favorite cities, for both climate and lifestyle choices.

Cutting off Ancestral Roots

What are the ancestral roots you want to cut and close the door on to keep from plaguing future generations? Many of us are unaware what some of our prior family members struggled with. We are not responsible for their sins, but they do affect our lives.

Example: when two single people, aged sixteen years old, have a child and have no family support, is it the child's fault what their parents did? Will that baby be affected by the teen parents' lack of maturity, funds, and ability to care for them?

Cutting ancestral roots can provide repentance, healing, and faith in many areas such as poverty, rejection, inferiority, abuse, divorce, addictions, control, strongholds, anger, offense, soul ties, violence, unforgiveness, vows, word curses, oppression/depressions, fear, doubts insecurity, shame, sexual promiscuity, abandonment, bitterness, or vows.

Battle Zone

1. What are the three key Ancestral Roots you want to cut off the family tree?

_____

_____

_____

_____

2. How can you cut the root from affecting your children and future?

_____

_____

_____

_____

_____

3. Why would these blessings be important for you?

_____

_____

_____

_____

_____

4. Why would it be important for children?

_____

_____

_____

_____

5.   Why would it be important for your

career?

_____

_____

_____

_____

_____

6.   Why would it be important for your

health?

_____

_____

_____

_____

_____

7.   Why would it be important for your
finances?

_____

_____

_____

_____

_____

8.   Why would it be important for you
emotionally?

_____

_____

_____

_____

_____

Ancestral Roots Cut Off

Don't pray the prayer below unless you are ready and believe.

Father God, the creator of Heaven and Earth, I stand before you on behalf of my family to break the generational patterns of sins and despair of _____, _____, _____. No longer shall this family line be held in bondage by sin. I repent to the son Jesus Christ who died for my sins and made all things new. I stand in repentance for family and my own personal sins of _____, _____, _____. Jesus, you are my Lord and Savior. I humbly ask for your forgiveness of our sins. I desire to live according to your word. I need you each day to guide, lead, and advise me. May I be granted all that I ask and long for in Jesus' name.

What's the blessing of your culture and heritage?

Chapter Ten

Love that Hurts - Soul Ties

Titus 3:1-5
"Remind the people to be subject to rulers and authorities, to be obedient, to be ready to do whatever is good, to slander no one, to be peaceable and considerate, and always to be gentle toward everyone.
At one time we too were foolish, disobedient, deceived and enslaved by all kinds of passions and pleasures. We lived in malice and envy, being hated and hating one another. But when the kindness and love of God our Savior appeared, he saved us, not because of righteous things we had done, but because of his mercy. He saved us through the washing of rebirth and renewal by the Holy Spirit."

Soul Ties

It would be very difficult to live in this world and not accumulate good and bad soul ties. No matter how perfect everyone looks and acts, somebody has done something to hurt your feelings or you have done the hurting. My experience with soul ties was breaking off the idolatry. You see anyone or anything that you love more than God is an idol.

Idolatry

I can think of a relationship that I was so blinded by love that nobody else mattered. I gave my whole heart and soul willingly, believing this person completed me. I believed this person had to be from God and would rescue me from a past of pain to a future of love and joy. I was disappointed, and they didn't come close to bringing the future of security and love I so desired.

Career

When I didn't find love and security in relationships, I moved on to the thing I could count on, myself. My career was something I could put my attention, discipline, and hard work into, achieving the shattering of the glass ceiling. That was disappointing when you must look at the politics, racism, and gender bias. I was left disappointed again.

I just named a few, but I could go on and on about things we put our trust in more than God. Idolatry is anything we worship more than God. For some of you, it's social media and your desperate needs for likes, fans, and followers. You want to be an idol. We even have a TV show called American Idol. Before we get to Soul Ties, you may want to look at the real reason you want to be idol and have people worship you.

Soul Tie

A soul tie (according to www.greatbiblestudy.com) in its simplest form ties two souls together in the spiritual realm for a godly or ungodly reason. Another way people discuss it is regarding sexual relations: married versus unmarried. Soul-ties can be to places and things as well. Everyone you have had sex with has created a soul tie with you. With divorce rates high, too many women today are left devastated from the emotions of Love and Lust.

When the relationship is over, many women feel the residue of sin in many areas, spiritually, emotionally, and physically. There is one area that is rarely discussed because it's a controversial subject matter.

How do you form soul ties?

Sexual relations - *Ephesians 5:31* discusses the godly soul tie. When a husband and a wife are joined together, they are in covenant and committed in holy matrimony.

However, when a person has sexual relations outside of marriage we go to *Galatians 5:19-21*

"Now the works of the flesh are evident: sexual immorality, impurity, sensuality, idolatry, sorcery, enmity, strife, jealousy, fits of anger, rivalries, dissensions, divisions, envy, drunkenness, orgies, and things like these. I warn you, as I warned you before, that those who do such things will not inherit the kingdom of God."

Love & Lust Connections- (Soul Ties)

The devil is always counterfeiting God's plans with promises of love, desire, and no restraint. That sounds good in the beginning until a woman connects sexually with a man that is not her husband and leads to heartache. Now the woman is connected in a spiritual, physical, and emotional way. Many don't know how to regain the fullness of their soul through repentance.

Why is that? Have you ever wondered why women seem to hang on to relationships a lot longer than men? Men have moved on to the next conquest while you are home watching reruns of The Way We Were and asking, "Why did this happen to me?"

There are a significant number of women left with not only a broken heart, but the soul tie seed of the man growing within their body. The original soul tie now has created a soul tie that binds the two people. There lies a decision to be made by a woman that will bring various levels of emotions that she may keep secret but will have an effect whether its acknowledged or not.

Soul Tie that Binds

A soul tie that is never discussed in the church is abortion. Most of abortions are not carried out by married couples but many Christian single women who hooked up for exciting sex that resulted in an emotional decision that lasted far longer than the man in many cases.

According to the Abortion World Clock

Below list how many babies were aborted in America and worldwide thus far in 2017. You may be saying, "Don't remind me, Lisa." We must deal with all things that hinder our future growth.

2017

US – 912,000

Worldwide – 40,000,000,

Since Roe vs. Wade

US – 60,000,000

US Black (since '73) – 18,000,000

You may find that you are a part of this statistic. However, you feel about the subject, this is still an incredible number of abortions. The goal of discussing the soul tie of abortion is the link between how a woman feels, deals, and heals emotionally after the abortion.

Whether you are for or against abortions has no bearing on this chapter. I am not here to challenge your decision or make a judgment. I think we can all agree the aftermath of the abortion decision can bring a range of emotions from relief to guilt, and/or depression.

I want women to gain healing if you have felt any of the below potential side effects of a past abortion. You might say I haven't had an abortion. That is great. You probably know women who have had and could use a wise female for support. If you believe in any form or manner the below emotions have affected you, it's time to let go of the soul tie and let God heal you. Many may ask, "Is forgiveness available to me?"

I can tell you it is. I have seen so many women delivered from the guilt, bitterness, anger, and shame over this subject matter.

Below is according to the American Pregnancy Association:

Potential side effects include:

- Regret
- Anger
- Guilt
- Shame
- Sense of loneliness or isolation
- Loss of self confidence
- Insomnia or nightmares
- Relationship issues
- Suicidal thoughts and feelings
- Eating disorders
- Depression
- Anxiety

Who's More Prone to Experience Emotional Side Effects?

It is possible for anyone to experience an unexpected emotional or psychological side effect following an abortion. Women commonly report that the abortion procedure affected them more than they expected. However, some individuals are more susceptible to experiencing some type of emotional or psychological struggle.

Women with a higher probability of having a negative emotional or psychological side effect include:

- Individuals with previous emotional or psychological concerns
- Individuals who have been coerced, forced, or persuaded to get an abortion
- Individuals with religious beliefs that conflict with abortion
- Individuals with moral or ethical views that conflict with abortion
- Individuals who obtain an abortion in the later stages of pregnancy

- Individuals without support from significant others or their partner
- Women obtaining an abortion for genetic or fetal abnormalities.

I once counseled a woman who had four abortions. The pregnancies were her affirmations if her boyfriends loved her or not. It was almost a test. She lived with a single mother who wasn't married and had children by men who didn't marry her. She thought if she got pregnant and the man married her, she would have found true love.

In her world, all women were single with kids they couldn't afford. She didn't know that her childhood fears, vows, and generational patterns were open doors leading her to test men by not using protection and caution as stringent as she should. Her low self-esteem and ideals led to continued disappointment.

The men felt trapped and gave her many reasons why she should have the abortions. They offered to marry her when the time was right, bought her things, and shared how they didn't want to limit their relationship. She, not wanting to ruin the men's lives, had the abortions reluctantly.

In later years, she regretted the abortions and realized the men used her sexually and never loved her or planned a future with her. She felt isolated and carried this secret of pain for many years. She decided to share with a fiancé, and he responded with harsh words.

This was devastating, and she never shared her abortion choice again with other men, Christians, or believers because she believed God would not forgive her either.

I'm glad to report not only did she receive healing, she is married. She and her husband are ministry leaders, and I was proud to be part of her healing process with the Lord. She has many gifts and talents that she offers to young women near and far.

Do you feel the need to ask forgiveness? This is by choice. Try in your group setting to share your personal experience. Share your emotions with a partner in the group. You are in a safe, secure environment.

The devil will make you feel you are the only one here who had an abortion. Based on the number above, one in three women have an abortion by age forty-five.

WHY LOVE HURTS (www.dailymail.co.uk)

Sex is one of our biggest preoccupations — causing thrills, heartache, and downright confusion. But until recently, exactly what happens in the brain during sex was something of a mystery to scientists. Now, however, American researchers have uncovered what goes on in a woman's head during an orgasm.

Scientists from Rutgers University, New Jersey, used scans to monitor women's brains during orgasm and found that different brain parts are activated when various parts of her body are aroused. They found that up to thirty different parts of the brain are activated, including those responsible for emotion, touch, joy, satisfaction, and memory. The scientists also found that two minutes before orgasm, the brain's reward centers become active. These are the areas usually activated when eating food and drinking.

A key hormone released during sex is oxytocin, also known as the "cuddle hormone." This lowers our defenses and makes us trust people more, says Dr. Arun Ghosh, a GP specializing in sexual health at the Spire Liverpool Hospital.

It's also the key to bonding, as it increases levels of empathy. Women produce more of this hormone, although it's not clear why, and this means they are more likely to let their guard down and fall in love with a man after sex.

However, the problem is that the body can't distinguish whether the person we're with is a casual fling or marriage material — oxytocin is released either way. So, while it might help you bond with the love of your life, it's also the reason you may feel so miserable when a short-term relationship ends.

Men, on the other hand, instead of getting a surge of bonding hormone receive a surge of simple pleasure.

"The problem is that when a man has an orgasm, the main hormone released is dopamine — the pleasure hormone. And this surge can be addictive," says Dr. Ghosh. That's why so many more men tend to suffer from sex addiction.

Your tongue nor your flesh can hide sexual interaction. For example: at the workplace during meetings, I could sense when married people were having an affair. Their bodies in the meetings can't resist the closeness, the eye glance, the curl of the mouth, the hand gesture of intimacy.

I almost felt like I could smell the fragrance of their sexual desire.

My point is you haven't been hiding anything. Only you believe the lie that nobody knows. Insecure people talk too much or brag too much about how other people think they are great. Listening to them makes you say, "What reality are they in?" You need a closer intimate relationship with God now.

Life isn't fair, ladies. God created us to have sex with our Adam and be satisfied. Men on the other hand don't have that oxytocin. This is very important information when discussing sex education with daughters and females struggling with heartache and woundedness.

Most women have no clue about oxytocin. *Hosea 4:6* says, *"My people are destroyed from lack of knowledge."* If you take away the value of Christian living by having sex before you are ready, it will lead to heartbreak for young women. When most women have sex, they are looking for a connection of some type, whether casual or long term. The hormone oxytocin doesn't recognize the difference in booty calls or marrying the love of your life.

Imagine every man you have had an orgasm with made a connection with thirty different parts of the brain; your emotions, touch, joy, satisfaction and memory. Don't think you've escaped because you didn't have an orgasm. The memory, touch, joy, satisfaction is hard to let go of when the relationship ends. Our daughters need to be educated about how to conduct themselves and manage relationships with the opposite sex.

Healing of Soul Ties

Healing and deliverance of soul ties can feel emotionally complicated. There are many people in healing that agree on four steps taken with a spiritually mature seasoned coach:

- Acknowledge the ungodly soul ties which leads to repentance
- Repent, release the person/s from your soul, memory, touch, joy, satisfaction
- Forgive them and yourself
- Fill yourself with God's Truth

You can do the above for soul ties forced upon you such as sexual abuse, molestation, and incest.

Godly Soul Ties

There are also Godly soul ties such as your parents, husband, God, children, grandchildren, and church. Each of these Godly soul ties can become ungodly if abuse or misuse of power is operating outside the Word. For example, if a child is abused emotionally, physically, or sexually. The church can be an ungodly soul tie if they are operating outside the Word. Cults and the money changers are obvious ones. Your husband can be a soul tie due to divorce or negative words spoken over you during your relationship.

The secret I learned about gaining victory over soul ties is admitting your responsibility before God, repenting, and asking forgiveness. I agree you can say the words, but true forgiveness is the foundation of breaking the soul ties. Forgiving yourself starts with you and Jesus in prayer. I want to give you the short, quickest way to get over deadbeat soul ties.

Love Lost

It took me over twenty years to get over a soul tie that was affecting every area of my life. When I learned about oxytocin, I was in search because this person felt like they were in my DNA. Other great men in my life didn't have a chance because in my memory, my body, mind and soul wanted the soul tie of my past.

Teen suicides could be reduced if someone shared the facts about sex. TV and the media teach sex is great and the more the merrier, which is not true no matter what your faith or religious beliefs are. I didn't have the knowledge or attend a church that taught on the subject. I attended and grew up in church and had no knowledge of how to break soul ties.

To be honest, I have been through the training and still didn't get this quick step. Jesus had to clear the scales off my eyes. Wishing people well after they have hurt you doesn't work. Releasing forgiveness for all the low, painful acts waged against you is a powerful moment that only God can heal.

When you have a history of painful relationships, normally healing takes time to be realized. Always remember healing is a fervent process. You must always check your heart, you're thinking, and your words in this area. Other people can trigger your pain, and the devil is always looking for an open door to bring someone in to finish the job. I prayed for God to show me men that were not for my good very early in the relationship.

In 2010, I prayed that prayer during a fast, and the Lord did exactly that. I was saved heartache and pain and gained my confidence and identity of what I was worth. Men also realized who I was and treated me accordingly.

I must say the men in the church were worse than the men in the world. The men in the world would tell me they didn't want to interfere with God and my faith. There were too many other women with no values they could get over on, both in church and out.

It was very disappointing to see and hear the heartache soul ties of young people and old folks in the church creating ungodly soul ties. Based on my personal experience and working with women the last ten years in healing and soul ties, I learned that when you open the door for ungodly soul ties, you open yourself to demonic attack whether in sickness, poverty, depression, suicide, abortion, abuse, addictions, divorce, and generational struggles with sex.

Let's finish Hosea 4:6. "Because you have rejected knowledge, I also reject you as my priests; because you have ignored the law of your God, I also will ignore your children.

My Soul Tie Healing

I suffered depression, loneliness, rejection, abandonment, suicidal thoughts, rage, and isolation due to a soul tie. I knew this person was the love of my life. We were going to be married and had planned our wedding. Two months before our wedding, it ended. It's a book to itself.

What I learned in healing was he was an idol in my life. My whole everything revolved on this man bringing me joy, satisfaction, children, safety, protection, and more. I didn't need God because in my mind, he fulfilled it all. Well, God couldn't have that if I were going to fulfill His purpose.

If you have been paying attention, the devil attacked me in this area as a young child. To solidify these emotions, the enemy needs to bring others in our lives that we trust, love, and depend on and then, BAM, hit you with the tricks of your past. Once he can reinforce your old insecurities, his fortress around you becomes stronger and higher.

Everyone you meet feels the concrete pain, sorrow, and mourning. The enemy makes you believe you need to keep it to yourself because of shame and fear of opinion. The truth is, he doesn't want you to discuss it because you will learn he does this to every woman and they will share how they overcame the pain. Secrets are a trap.

Generational Soul Ties

When I searched and learned the history of my mother and grandmother's soul ties, I saw the pattern that I had to break. You must ask questions if you don't know your family history. Remember the scripture on knowledge. We must seek it out.

Breaking soul ties changes not only your life, but your children's and generations to come. If teen pregnancy is in your family generationally and caused deep wounds from soul ties, it is about time your children have healthy relationships. Get your full heart back and live with the knowledge and truth of who deserves it all ... Jesus. Decide to be wise and disciplined in your thinking and in your body. Understand and teach your daughters the facts of life honestly.

There are ladies, and sisters, that God has surrounded you with that can help you expose the lie that this only happens or happened to you. It may feel difficult, but I promise you, saying it in front of strangers is easier. In weekly sessions, you are normally not in a group with people you know very well. Once you say it (you may cry, so what?), your freedom will begin.

Battle Zone

1. The first step is acknowledging your worship and/or belief in an idol over God, Jesus, and the Holy Spirit. Take a moment and repent. List your idols below:

_____

_____

_____

_____

_____

2. Examples of various prayer you can use or just talk to God in your own words: *Father, I repent for having an abortion which has led to the feelings of:*

_____

_____

_____

_____

_____

Jesus, forgive me...
Jesus, heal me...
Jesus, thank you for the healing of...
Three Steps to Freedom & Healing
Father, I acknowledge the ungodly soul ties with

_____.

I ask to no longer be connected in the spirit,

physically, emotionally, nor in the flesh to these
individuals. I have sinned before You, God, and I
repent. Release my mind, body, and soul from
this painful pattern. Renew my mind and soul
with the discipline, discernment, and characters
of a Warrior Women today for Jesus.
Today I ask to forgive

---

for engaging in sexual sin outside of covenant.
I release and break all connections to my flesh,
mind, joy, memory, pain, sadness, broken dreams,
condemnation, and dreams. I am free and close
all doors to the devil to harm me and my family
and generations to come.
I am made whole today and profess Jesus is
the son of God. I am loved, healed, and set
free this day in Jesus' name.

Chapter Eleven

Take Back Your Future

I want to share some final scriptures with you before I share encouraging words and how you and I can continue this journey together.

Hebrews 4:16

"Let us approach God's throne of grace with confidence, so that we may receive mercy and find grace to help us in our time of need."

Philippians 4:6-7

"Do not be anxious about anything, but in every situation, by prayer and petition, with thanksgiving, present your request to God. And the peace of God, which transcends all understanding, will guard your hearts and your minds in Christ Jesus."

Deuteronomy 31:6 (CSB)

"Be strong and courageous; don't be terrified or afraid of them. For the Lord your God is the one who will go with you; he will not leave you or abandon you."

I want to first thank you for having the courage to make the choice to join the battle for the kingdom of God. This is the first book of a three-part series on the journey to gaining access to God through faith and trust. My role was to introduce you to the Lord. I am a flawed woman just like you. I have had many challenges. I decided to get up when I fell, so I advise you to do the same.

We have many struggles in this life that leave us empty, abandoned, and alone. My prayer is that through each chapter, you've learned that you have never been alone. From before the womb, you were predestined.

This book challenged you to take key steps:

- Make the choice to serve God
- Acknowledge needing God's grace
- Cast all your cares to God through faith
- Be confident in your identity
- Your words have power
- Be strong, courageous, and fearless from the Word
- Remove idols from your life
- Be a daughter of the Most High God
- Begin the Warrior Women journey

My role is to facilitate you to the truth. The journey is not finished but just beginning for you. My purpose for the series of books is to be obedient to God and rejoice at the change that has begun in your life. I can only lead you by faith in the Word and help you with the Holy Spirit. You must do the work and fight for your life on the journey to see the fruit bloom.

You cannot win the war alone behind a fake smile, lipstick, heels, and designer clothes. You must be united in love with other women and the support provided for the Christian Warrior Women: Take Back Your Faith, Family & Future website, video and live speaking engagements.

Communicating with Me

You are blessed and have so much power from God to be displayed. I want to support your rise from the ashes to the precious sparkling diamond God has blessed.

I would love to come speak at your women's conference, church, or healing service. I have been doing this throughout the United States as well as internationally for the last seven years. I love seeing the power of God heal those who believe and trust him.

Feel free to email or contact me directly at www.LisaHawkinsauthor.com or www.christianwarriorwomen.com and on social media to answer questions or support your women's group community. Review the book on Amazon so other women can be set free. Please share your testimonies with me of how God used the book to bless you. In this first book, you get a clear picture of the Holy Spirit gifting and operating in my life. If I can serve your ministry or community, to inspire and motivate women to seek, wisdom, and knowledge of our Savior's love, I am open to your request based on availability.

Continue the Journey

If you have gained a new perspective and need help and support in growth on this path, then make sure you move on to Book Two of the series. All the updates on the series will be on the web, blog, and social media. Sign up so you can be on the team that inspires areas to include in the series.

I want to hear your testimonies of how God is changing your life due to this first book. Please share and encourage other women to be bold, courageous, and full of faith. We are at a time in history where we can stand confidently with Jesus or look at the past with regret. The milk spilled; clean it up and start again.

I want each of you to find five women and tell them about or gift them this book. Watch God move in their lives. If you want to be obedient to the Word in loving your neighbors, then you must be interested in their eternal soul. You don't need to do anything but write a message in the front of the book that states, "I bought you a gift that will bring peace to your life."

There is no pressure on you. God will have them read the book, and He will do the rest. Imagine how personal and engaging your relationship could become with this group of women. You will make an impact. When a woman is hungry, you feed her with the Word.

Maybe you know women who are struggling in their lives as a single parent, or with addictions. God will bless your efforts. I want to know the miracles you are bringing forth by sharing your healing and relationship with God.

God created women special among all the creations on the earth. We deserve to honor one another in His love, sacrifice, and death. As He resurrected His body on earth through the Holy Spirit, He can resurrect your heart, soul, and health to be a new creature with a new mindset and lifestyle. Join me in taking back all that's been robbed, stolen, and destroyed in your life.

Prayer

My prayer is that each day your faith grows, and you see the power of God activated in your life, workplace, and friends. You are the catalyst of change in the midst of the struggle. Be lifted with new armor that stretches your faith, courage, strength, and endurance to finish this life with a boldness in Jesus.

My prayer is that each chapter provided the opportunity to gain insight into your identity, relationship with God, uniting with other women for healing, and examining your behavior. You can learn and heal with women from all walks of life.

Encouraging Word

The prior chapters made you face your fears and demons. It also served to remind you where God has been in your life thus far. Understanding your mindset, behavior, and results gave you the opportunity to make a choice. This first book in the series is all about your choice.

Blaming others for where you are is a waste of time. Examining where you are in faith and identity will yield fruit for your future. Your choice to seek, repent, pray, and receive revelation develops a renewed mind to defend the faith and win the war. I look forward to talking with each of you on social media, emails, and in person. My joy comes from hearing, witnessing, and seeing God change the lives of His anointed, appointed daughters.

Remember, you didn't get these challenges or struggles overnight, so you must allow healing to take time, as well. The investment is in yourself. I look forward to meeting you, answering questions, and supporting your journey to Jesus through your workplace, small group, church, or other organization. Jesus is for all, so Christian Warrior Women ministers to all in need of healing and a fresh start. The tools and instructions are from God to you.

Will it be difficult and a challenge? You bet.

Renewed

You should be feel renewed, restored, and fully charged with the power of God. It's time to commit to affirming your new identity in faith and shaping your environment to new heights in Jesus' name. Your relationships, your marriage, your children, your workplace, your friends will be shocked and encouraged by the new you.

This first book wasn't about addressing every area of hurt. God revealed in this book your top wounds and insecurities to deal with now. I look forward to you continuing the journey with us in the series. He also gave you His armor to war with.

You must commit to the discipline, training, and your relationship with God. Don't read a chapter once and think that's all you'll need. Stay in the key chapters and wait on the Lord to bring change. There will be highs and lows, but He will see you through.

You will experience healing with a group of women and me that will produce a sisterhood, unity, and trust that will yield a community of faith. This book is a reminder to you each year to revisit your emotional health through your identity and actions. This isn't about making lists or a vision board about your fantasies. If you are serious about finding God, then your next step is going through the series of books and attending Warrior Women conferences with your small group. Finding the Lord is a time full of joy, tears, and laughter.

You will gain strength each day and motivate other women to try God in your community, church, and workplace. You will have a new heart, new spirit, and new purpose from God. There will be videos, a website, and at the end, a feast to celebrate with family and friends. My desire is to meet many of you and hear how you got over and onto God's path for your life. You must make the choice to be a Warrior Woman today!

Prophetic Word

I happened to visit a church that I had served on the healing and miracles team for years. This church had encouraged and mentored me in healing and prophecy when they saw God using me in their ministry.

I went up for a prophetic word, and Pastor Samuel went through training with me (he wasn't the Pastor then) and another woman (who had given me a prophetic word back in 2010) were waiting to pray for me. They did not know about Warrior Women or my plans.

I had the audio below transcribed. You will hear that God sent me a prophet to confirm what Warrior Women is all about. I pray each of you grab hold to what God is doing in this hour with the women of God.

Pastor Samuel Word: "This is for Lisa, Lisa Hawkins. Daughter, this is an hour where I'm breathing a fresh wind toward you, the winds of change are blowing, they are blowing, they're blowing. For I'm bringing a new mindset to you, I'm bringing a new level of thinking, I'm bringing a new level of understanding, for I'm bringing understanding toward the things of the kingdom.

I'm giving you an understanding of how I operate as the Father. Even as you have seen a trickle of it, I will begin to show you even more how when I say a thing, it will hasten to you and it will even run you down to pursue you to overtake you. When I send blessings toward you, so know that in this hour I will begin to show you who you need to align yourself with and who you need to separate from, who needs to be around you for I am bringing you as a change agent.

For I'm breathing change into you and breathing change around you, as well. Know that I will bring those around you to mentor. I will bring those around you that need to sup with me. For you will show them how to gain access to the things of the kingdom and know that as I am increasing your level of sensitivity for the things of the Spirit, I'm sharpening your eyesight, I'm sharpening your perception, I am sharpening even your level of discernment.

For you will begin to see the enemy afar off, then you will sound an alarm that the warriors of God will begin to know and understand that this is a time of warfare. Even as Nehemiah was able to build the wall, he had his weapon of warfare in the other hand as he built it, and when the enemy showed his face he began to sound the alarm and the men of God. The warriors of God began to surround and began to protect.

You will be one that I will begin to show where the enemy is about to pop his head up, and you will sound the alarm. It will be the alarm of the warriors and the warriors of God will raise up and the intercessors of God will raise up and the watchmen will begin to raise up and there will be a greater level of authority and anointing that you will walk in. Know that you have not seen the greatest days of my outpouring yet. For I am pouring into you a deeper level of understanding revelation, but even a deeper level of signs and wonders.

For even as you have a heart for me, I am raising even your appetite for the things of me, so you'll begin to thirst, hunger, you will begin to hunger harder. I will fill you even faster and give you more capacity to walk in the things of the kingdom. Know that the kingdom is not a far-off thing. For you, I am bringing you right face to face with the kingdom, and it will be a daily existence and a daily lifestyle that you will lead and walk in.

Know that as you have been successful in other things, I am bringing success for the things of the kingdom. There will be a calling card that will go out to the places that you are to go for your name will precede you. For they will know that you walk in me, and you know that I walk in you. For now, is an hour of expansion. Expansion as I am breathing new life and changes coming around you. I am also expanding some things business-wise and for the things of the kingdom.

For you will find yourself teaching, you will find yourself mentoring, you'll find yourself training for these are the things that I will activate you into more in a faster way. For knowing the next three to six months, you're going to find yourself training, you are going to find yourself teaching. Know that I am bringing you into a place of proper positioning where I'm aligning all things. You will be activated to go forth with liberty to minister and to teach and to train and to mentor and to raise up another generation of kingdom women that know how to go forward in the things of God."

Last Word

Again, I hope the first book in the series- *Christian Warrior Women: Taking Back Your Faith, Family & Future* gave you the support needed to shed light into a dark place in your life. God led you to the series of books, now you must choose to use the weapons of warfare.

If you do what you always did, you will get what you always got.

-Anonymous

Success is walking from failure to failure with no loss of enthusiasm.

-Winston Churchill

Famous Woman Quote

A woman is like a tea bag - you can't tell how strong she is until you put her in hot water. ...

For more Inspirational and motivational material, please visit our website
@
www.lisahawkinsauthor.com
www.christianwarriorwomen.com

you can also like us on Facebook
@
https://www.facebook.com/LisaHawkinsauthor/

Made in the USA
Middletown, DE
21 August 2018